Study Guide

MULTINATIONAL FINANCIAL MANAGEMENT

Study Guide

Andrea L. DeMaskey
Villanova University

FIFTH EDITION

MULTINATIONAL FINANCIAL MANAGEMENT

ALAN C. SHAPIRO

 PRENTICE HALL, Upper Saddle River, New Jersey 07458

Production Editor: *Joseph F. Tomasso*
Acquisitions Editor: *Paul Donnelly*
Associate Editor: *Teresa Cohan*
Manufacturing Buyer: *Vincent Scelta*

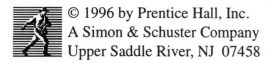 © 1996 by Prentice Hall, Inc.
A Simon & Schuster Company
Upper Saddle River, NJ 07458

Printed in the United States of America

10   9   8   7   6   5   4   3   2   1

I S B N   0 - 1 3 - 2 3 8 3 2 0 - 9

Prentice-Hall International (UK) Limited, *London*
Prentice-Hall of Australia Pty. Limited, *Sydney*
Prentice-Hall Canada Inc., *Toronto*
Prentice-Hall Hispanoamericana, S.A., *Mexico*
Prentice-Hall of India Private Limited, *New Delhi*
Prentice-Hall of Japan, Inc., *Tokyo*
Simon & Schuster Asia Pte. Ltd., *Singapore*
Editora Prentice-Hall do Brasil, Ltda., *Rio de Janiero*

CONTENTS OF THE STUDY GUIDE

PREFACE

The purpose of this *Study Guide* is to help you develop an understanding of the conceptual framework within which the key financial decisions of multinational corporations can be analyzed.

This *Study Guide* follows the chapter outline of *Multinational Financial Management, Fifth Edition*. In each chapter of the *Study Guide* you will find a chapter overview, a chapter outline and exercises consisting of fill-in-the-blanks, conceptual questions, and problems for study purposes.

I have tried to make this *Study Guide* as clear and error-free as possible. However, mistakes do occur, and there are almost certainly sections that could be further clarified and refined. Thus, any suggestions for improving this *Study Guide* would be greatly appreciated.

Andrea L. DeMaskey
Villanova University

January 1996

CHAPTER 1

INTRODUCTION: MULTINATIONAL ENTERPRISE AND MULTINATIONAL FINANCIAL MANAGEMENT

Overview

Doing business internationally is not new. For thousands of years, nations have been transferring goods and services across their borders. With the end of World War II, however, international business became increasingly important and with it the multinational corporation. The tremendous market potential which opened up in Western Europe and the vast amount of untapped resources and the availability of lower cost production facilities in the Asian countries attracted, and continue to attract, many firms to enter foreign markets. To take advantage of these opportunities, companies first begin by exporting before setting up production sites abroad, which is the last step in the globalization process. Regardless of the foreign entry strategy, a true multinational corporation is one which is committed to seek out, undertake, and integrate production, marketing, R&D, and financing opportunities on a global, not domestic, scale.

Faced with these opportunities and the unique risks of operating internationally, the decisions made by the financial manager must be consistent with the goal of the firm. The primary objective of multinational financial management is the maximization of shareholder wealth. Other financial goals reflect management's relative autonomy and pressures imposed by the host environment. Thus, the financial policies of domestic firms must be modified to reflect the additional risks and rewards of being multinational. The theoretical foundation of international finance can be found in the concepts of arbitrage, market efficiency, and capital asset pricing. Purely financial measures, however, will not increase the value of the firm. Rather, the financial executive must be aware of capital market imperfections and differences in tax regulations to enhance the value of good financial management.

Outline

I. **International business has undergone revolutionary changes out of which has emerged the multinational corporation.**

A. A multinational corporation is a company with production and distribution facilities in more than one country. It consists of a parent company located in the home country and at least five or six foreign affiliates.

B. The classical theory of international trade, which was first developed by Adam Smith and David Ricardo, did not anticipate the rise of the multinational corporation.
1. This theory, based on the doctrine of comparative advantage, states that each nation should specialize in producing and exporting those goods that it can produce most efficiently and import those goods that other nations can produce most efficiently.
2. The ability of multinational corporations to move certain factors of production internationally outweigh the macroeconomic differences among countries, as postulated by Smith and Ricardo.

3. The traditional world economy of exporting has been replaced by one in which value is added in different countries through differences in costs and skills among nations.

C. Fundamental political, technological, regulatory, and economic forces can radically change the global competitive environment.

D. Firms become multinational by moving overseas for the following reasons.
  1. Raw material seekers exploit the materials that can be found in foreign countries.
  2. Market seekers produce and sell in foreign markets.
  3. Cost minimizers seek out and invest in lower-cost production facilities abroad.

II. **The process of overseas expansion typically begins with exporting followed by setting up local production facilities or licensing.**

A. To remain competitive, members of oligopolistic industries both create and take advantage of product and factor market imperfections internationally. At the same time, they try to reduce the perceived competitive threats posed by other members in the same industry.

B. The globalization of a firm takes place in phases moving from a relatively low risk/low return, export-oriented strategy to a higher risk/higher return strategy emphasizing overseas production facilities.

C. Exporting is a preferred market entry strategy for firms faced with highly uncertain demand abroad.
  1. Advantages: (a) Low capital requirements and start-up costs; (b) low risk followed by immediate returns; (c) great opportunity to learn about present and future supply and demand conditions, competition, channels of distribution, financial institutions and techniques.
  2. Disadvantages: (a) Inability to realize the full sales potential of a product.
  3. As uncertainty is reduced and success builds, firms begin to deal directly with foreign agents and distributors rather than using an export agent. They may also set up sales subsidiaries and new service facilities to be controlled by the firms themselves.

D. Establishing production facilities abroad demonstrates greater commitment to the local market.
  1. Advantages: (a) Increased sales volume; (b) increased assurance of supply stability; (c) direct control over the production process and the distribution system; (d) more comprehensive service and support to the local customers.
  2. Disadvantages: (a) Increased risk due to (1) differing tax laws; (2) government regulations; (3) exchange rate volatility.
  3. A firm can set up local production by acquiring an existing business or building its own facility.

E. Licensing offers an alternative to producing overseas through an affiliate. Under a licensing arrangement, a local firm agrees to manufacture the company's products for royalties and other forms of payment.
  1. Advantages: (a) Minimum investment outlay; (b) faster to enter the foreign market; (c) fewer financial and legal risks.
  2. Disadvantages: (a) Low profits; (b) difficulty in maintaining product quality standards; (c) problems controlling exports by the foreign licensee; (d) loss of potential revenues resulting from a strong competitive position of the licensee once the licensing agreement has expired.

F. From a behavioral viewpoint, the true multinational corporation can be defined in terms of its commitment to seeking out, undertaking, and integrating investment, marketing and financing opportunities on a global, not domestic, scale.

G. To remain competitive internationally, the global manager must be able to understand political and economic differences; search for the most cost-effective mix of supplies, components, distribution systems and funds; identify its alternatives; and evaluate how the value of the firm will be affected by their changing relative values

H. As the integration of national economies continues, politicians must accept the reality of a global economy or watch their countries fall behind.

III. **Multinational corporations are faced with many opportunities and are subjected to unique risks. To properly balance these international risks and returns, the fundamental concepts of domestic corporate finance must be modified.**

A. The goal of multinational financial management is to maximize shareholder wealth which translates into maximizing the price per share of the company.

B. Other financial goals reflect the multinational corporation's ability to shift money and profits among its various foreign affiliates.
   1. Through internal transfer mechanisms, such as transfer pricing, intercorporate loans, dividend payments, leading and lagging intercorporate payments, and fees and royalties, firms can minimize their risks and maximize global profits.
   2. In addition, multinational corporations have greater control over the transfer mode and the timing of their financial transactions.
   3. Since multinational corporations are able to avoid taxes and regulatory barriers through the use of these internal transfer mechanisms, conflicts with nation-states will arise.

C. While the international financial executive makes both investment and financing decisions as his/her domestic counterpart, he/she is faced with added political and economic risks as well as more complex tax laws and multiple financial markets.

D. The benefits of operating globally include accessing segmented capital markets, moving funds to lower tax countries, and taking advantage of international diversification and lower cost production sites.

E. Financial economics, which utilizes economic analysis to understand the behavior of financial markets, offers valuable insights for the international financial manager.

F. The following three basic concepts provide the theoretical foundation for the study of international corporate finance:
   1. Arbitrage arises when price differences exist in two separate markets. In this case, securities or commodities are bought in one market and sold immediately in the other market to profit from the price discrepancy. A multinational corporation can engage in (a) tax arbitrage in which it is taking advantage of different tax rates; and (b) risk arbitrage or speculation in which it takes advantage of differing returns adjusted for risk on different financial securities.
   2. Market efficiency ensures that traded securities are priced fairly. In an efficient market, new information is readily reflected in the prices of securities.

3. Capital asset pricing refers to the way in which securities are valued with regard to their risks and expected returns. The capital asset pricing model (CAPM) assumes that total risk can be divided into two parts: (a) diversifiable (unsystematic or company-specific) risk, and (b) nondiversifiable (systematic or market) risk.

G. Total risk can adversely affect the value of a firm by leading to lower sales and higher costs. Thus, any company which takes actions that decrease its total risk will improve its sales and cost outlook, thereby increasing its expected cash flows.

H. Financial markets continually judge a nation's economic policies which is readily reflected in the determination of the value of its currency.

I. International financial managers can create value by taking advantage of capital market imperfections and tax asymmetries.

IV. **The organization of international financial management focuses on those areas in which financial decisions can have a substantial impact on the value of the firm.**

A. In order to make sound financial decisions internationally, the financial executive must understand the environment in which the MNC and its affiliates operate. In Chapter 2, the determination of exchange rates is examined. Chapter 3 describes the official part of the international financial system, and Chapter 4 analyzes the balance of payments and its linkages to national economies. Chapters 5 and 6 describe the functioning of the foreign exchange markets, including foreign currency futures and options markets. The five key equilibrium relationships in international finance are introduced in Chapter 7.

B. The multinational financial manager has to realize that the presence of his/her company in a number of countries and the diversity of its operations provide challenges as well as opportunities. Chapters 8 through 11 analyze the measurement and management of foreign exchange rate risk.

C. Most of the financial decisions relate to the current, on-going operations of the multinational corporation. Chapters 12 and 13 deal with the management of current liabilities, including a discussion on trade financing. In addition, international financial managers must ensure that cash, inventory, and receivables are used most effectively, as described in Chapters 14 and 15.

D. The multinational capital budgeting decision process is analyzed in Chapters 16 through 21. Because of the added political and economic risks and multiple tax regulations, the foreign investment analysis is more complex. These variables must be identified, measured, and incorporated into the capital budgeting analysis.

E. Once the foreign investment decision has been made, the financial manager has to decide on the most favorable financing package. Chapters 22 through 24 evaluate the financing alternatives which are available. These include the foreign capital markets, foreign bond markets, foreign equity markets and the international capital markets; namely, the Eurocurrency and Eurobond markets. In addition, the multinational corporation can finance its operations with interest rate and currency swaps or debt-equity swaps.

F. The expansion of banks into foreign markets and the development of the international debt crisis are discussed in Chapter 25. Chapter 26 shows how country risk can be evaluated.

V. Particularly with the end of World War II, U.S. firms have made substantial investments abroad. This trend subsided with the onset of the debt crisis in the early 1980s. The U.S. itself has also become an attractive source of foreign direct investment. The size and scope of overseas investment by U.S. firms and U.S. investment by foreign firms as well as its implications on sovereign states is discussed in Appendix 1A.

Fill-in-the-Blanks

1. The _____ _____ is a company which is engaged in the production and sale of goods and services in numerous countries.

2. According to the _____ _____ __ _____ _____ each country should specialize in making only those goods that can be produced relatively efficiently.

3. The existence of the multinational corporation is based on the _____ _____ of certain factors of production.

4. Multinational firms can be classified as _____ _____ _____, _____ _____, or _____ _____.

5. _____ ___ _____ _____ provide opportunities to multinational corporations to outcompete local firms, particularly those in _____ industries.

6. The _____ of _____ _____ ordinarily evolves from a risk-minimizing strategy to a higher return strategy.

7. Usually, the sequence of foreign expansion begins with _____ followed by _____ _____ _____ and at times _____ as a precursor to setting up production facilities abroad.

8. The distinguishing element of the multinational corporation is its commitment to _____ ___, _____, and _____ manufacturing, marketing, R&D, and financing opportunities on a worldwide, not domestic, scale.

9. By using _____ _____ _____, such as transfer pricing, intercompany loans, dividend payments and leading and lagging, a multinational corporation can maximize global profits. In addition, it is able to control the _____ and _____ of these internal financial transactions.

10. _____ between the MNC and the host government arise because taxes and other regulatory barriers can be avoided by moving funds among the MNC's several foreign units.

11. While MNCs are faced with added _____ and _____ ____, they benefit from the many _____ associated with operating internationally.

12. In developing a theoretical foundation for the study of international finance, three basic concepts in financial economics have proven to be of particular importance: _____, _____ _____, and _____ _____ _____.

13. The _____ of the firm can be _____ only if financial managers can take advantage of capital market imperfections and tax asymmetries.

Conceptual Questions

14. The primary objective of multinational financial management is to maximize global profits.
    a. True
    b. False

15. Which category of multinational is Texas Instruments most likely to fall in?
    a. Raw material seeker
    b. Market seeker
    c. Cost minimizer
    d. All of the above
    e. None of the above

16. The multinational financial system enables companies to
    a. circumvent currency controls.
    b. reduce taxes.
    c. access lower cost financing sources.
    d. all of the above.
    e. none of the above.

17. Multinational corporations are riskier than purely domestic firms.
    a. True
    b. False

18. The globalization process tends to proceed in a preprogrammed series of steps.
    a. True
    b. False

Answers

1. multinational corporation

2. classical theory of international trade

3. international mobility

4. raw material seekers; market seekers; cost minimizers

5. Product and market imperfections; oligopolistic

6. process; international expansion

7. exporting; foreign sales subsidiaries; licensing

8. seeking out; undertaking; integrating

9. internal transfer mechanisms; mode; timing

10. Conflicts

11. political; economic risks; opportunities

12. arbitrage; market efficiency; capital asset pricing

13. value; maximized

14. **b.** The primary objective of multinational financial management is the maximization of shareholder wealth.

15. **c.** Texas Instruments is a company which seeks out and invests in lower-cost production sites overseas to remain cost competitive both at home and abroad.

16. **d.** The multinational financial system enables corporations to circumvent exchange controls, reduce taxes, and gain access to lower-cost financing.

17. **b.** Multinational firms may be less risky than domestic firms if the added risks of operating abroad are more than offset by the ability to operate in countries whose economic cycles are not perfectly in phase.

18. **b.** The globalization process is the unplanned result of a series of corporate responses to a variety of threats and opportunities appearing at random.

CHAPTER 2

THE DETERMINATION OF EXCHANGE RATES

Overview

Without any government intervention, exchange rates are determined by the free interplay of supply and demand. Exchange rates, in turn, are affected by relative inflation rates, relative interest rates, and relative income levels. Monetary policy plays an important role here. If the money supply is expanded at a faster rate than the money demand, the domestic inflation rate will increase, and the domestic currency will depreciate. In addition, a strong currency is the result of a healthy economy. Exchange rates are also affected by expectations about future exchange rate changes which, in turn, depend on forecasts of future economic and political conditions.

Governments intervene in the foreign exchange market to achieve certain economic or political objectives. This can be accomplished either by affecting the market demand for and market supply of two currencies or by controlling the exchange rate directly.

Currencies are nonconvertible paper money; that is, a currency's value is not tied to a commodity such as gold. As a result, people are not sure what to expect, and any new information will dramatically affect their beliefs which, in turn, causes exchange rates to be rather volatile.

Outline

I. **An equilibrium exchange rate is the price at which currency supply equals currency demand.**

    A. The demand for a foreign currency is derived from the demand for that country's goods, services, and financial assets.

    B. The supply of a foreign currency is derived from that country's demand for foreign goods, services, and financial assets.

    C. As more goods and services are demanded from a foreign country, the price of the foreign currency will tend to increase. Conversely, as foreigners demand more foreign goods and services, the price of the foreign currency will tend to decrease.

    D. When country A's currency becomes more valuable relative to country B's currency, country A's currency is said to appreciate relative to that of country B, and country B's currency is said to depreciate relative to that of country A.
       1. The amount of foreign currency appreciation (depreciation) is computed as the fractional increase or decrease in the dollar value of a foreign currency.

$$(e_1 - e_0)/e_0$$

2. The amount of dollar appreciation (depreciation) is computed as the fractional decrease or increase in the foreign currency value of the dollar.

$$(e_0 - e_1)/e_1$$

3. For example, an increase in the pound from $1.50 to $1.54 is equivalent to a pound appreciation of 2.67% [(1.54 - 1.50)/1.50] or a dollar depreciation of 2.60% [(1.50 - 1.54)/1.54].

E. The movement of exchange rates is affected by inflation rates, interest rates, and GNP growth rates.
   1. If the rate of inflation in country A is higher than in country B, country A's currency is likely to depreciate relative to that of country B's.
   2. If the interest rate in country A is higher than in country B, country A's currency will tend to appreciate relative to that of country B.
   3. If country A's rate of economic growth is higher than that of country B, country A's currency is expected to appreciate.
   4. If a nation is more politically and economically stable, its currency is regarded to be of low risk and is more highly valued by investors than high-risk currencies.

II. **Like other financial markets, the foreign exchange market reacts to any news that may have a future effect.**

A. If currencies are viewed as financial assets, then the exchange rate is the relative price of two financial assets, which will be influenced by expectations of future economic, political and social factors. The price of a foreign currency, in turn, is determined by the demand for and supply of foreign-currency denominated assets. This approach to exchange rate determination is known as the asset market model.

B. The demand for money depends on its usefulness as a store of value, the demand for liquidity, as well as on its demand for assets denominated in that currency.

C. According to the asset market model, a nation's currency tends to strengthen with sound economic policies.

D. Exchange rates will also be influenced by the expectations of central bank behavior.
   1. High-quality currencies are those expected to maintain their purchasing power because they are issued by reputable central banks.
   2. Central bank independence can help establish a sound monetary policy which, in turn, increases the value of a nation's currency.
   3. Some countries have established a currency board that operates without discretionary monetary policies and without the existence of a central bank. Countries participating in this system have the same inflation rate as the country issuing the reserve currency and successfully maintain convertibility at a fixed exchange rate into the reserve currency.

E. The value of a country's currency can be depressed if its monetary policies are uncertain and incredible.

III. Central banks intervene in the foreign exchange market by buying or selling foreign currencies.

A. As the real or inflation-adjusted exchange rate rises by more than is necessary to offset the inflation differential between two countries, the domestic price of goods increases relative to the foreign price of goods.

B. The rise in the value of the U.S. dollar causes domestic customers to buy more foreign goods at lower prices while, at the same time, U.S. exports become less competitive worldwide. A fall in the value of the U.S. dollar improves U.S. exports but increases the price of foreign goods to domestic customers. Consequently, they will buy less thereby eroding their standard of living.

C. Governments intervene in the foreign exchange market to influence their currencies.
   1. If the central bank intervenes in the foreign exchange market without adjusting the money supply for exchange rate changes, it is engaging in unsterilized intervention.
   2. If the central bank intervenes in the foreign exchange market and desires to retain the dollar money supply, it uses sterilized intervention, which is accomplished with simultaneous transactions in the foreign exchange market and the Treasury securities market.

D. Intervention in the currency market to control the value of a currency tends to be either ineffectual or irresponsible.

E. Foreign exchange market intervention can have a lasting effect on exchange rate changes only if it causes permanent changes in relative money supplies.

F. Empirical evidence indicates that real exchange rates are primarily a function of real economic variables, such as relative national income levels and interest rates between currencies. Real exchange rates also determine the amount and the directional flows of goods, services, and capital among countries.

IV. According to the equilibrium approach to exchange rates, currency supply and currency demand are balanced through price adjustments.

A. The disequilibrium theory of exchange rates states that nominal exchange rate changes caused by monetary shocks will lead to real exchange rate changes, because prices in the goods and currency markets adjust at different speeds. It can also lead to exchange rate overshooting whereby short-term changes in the exchange rate exceed long-term changes in the equilibrium exchange rate.

B. The equilibrium theory, which is based on market clearing through price adjustments, suggests that relative price changes, including exchange rates, are caused by real shocks to the supply or demand in the goods market.

C. There are three important implications for exchange rates.
   1. Changes in relative prices are not caused by exchange rates; rather, relative price changes and real exchange rate changes occur simultaneously, and both are influenced by more fundamental economic variables.
   2. Governments will be unsuccessful if they try to affect real exchange rates through currency market intervention.
   3. No simple relationship exists between real exchange rate changes and changes in international competitiveness, employment, and the trade balance.

    D. Empirical evidence has shown that real exchange rate changes tend to persist for long periods of time. Nominal exchange rate changes were also found to be largely permanent.

Fill-in-the-Blanks

1. Exchange rates are _____-_____ _____ which are determined by the supply of and demand for foreign currencies.

2. A nation's currency _____ with inflation.

3. Higher _____ _____ will cause a country's currency to appreciate.

4. Since a stronger economy attracts capital, economic growth should lead to a _____ currency.

5. The value of a currency also depends on _____ of future economic, political, and social factors.

6. According to the ____ _____ ____, the exchange rate between two currencies is the price which equilibrates the supply of and the demand for assets denominated in those currencies.

7. The ____ _____ _____ is measured as the nominal exchange rate adjusted for changes in the relative price levels.

8. Central banks intervene in the currency market by _____ and _____ foreign exchange to influence their currencies.

9. ____ _____ _____ will affect the exchange rate in the same way as _____ intervention.

10. Based on the _____ _____ to exchange rates, currency markets clear through price adjustments.

Conceptual Questions

11. If a foreigner purchases a U.S. government security,
    a. the supply of dollars rises.
    b. the federal government deficit declines.
    c. the demand for dollars rises.
    d. the U.S. money supply rises.
    e. none of the above.

12. Which of the following is an example of direct intervention in the foreign exchange market?
    a. Lowering interest rates
    b. Increasing the discount rate
    c. Exchanging dollars for foreign currency
    d. Imposing barriers on international trade
    e. None of the above

13. The Fed adopts an easier monetary policy. As a result, the value of the dollar and U.S. interest rates will rise.
    a. True
    b. False

Problems

14. Suppose the Mexican peso devalues by 75% against the U.S. dollar. What is the percentage appreciation of the U.S. dollar against the peso?
    a. 25%
    b. 75%
    c. 300%
    d. 3%
    e. none of the above

15. Suppose the U.S. dollar appreciated by 500% against the Brazilian cruzado. By how much has the cruzado devalued against the U.S. dollar?
    a. 83.33%
    b. 500%
    c. 600%
    d. 800%
    e. none of the above

Answers and Solutions

1. market-clearing prices

2. depreciates

3. interest rates

4. stronger

5. expectations

6. asset market model

7. real exchange rate

8. buying; selling

9. Open market operations; unsterilized

10. equilibrium approach

11. **c.** To purchase U.S. government securities, foreigners must pay for them in U.S. dollars. As they exchange their currencies for U.S. dollars, the demand for U.S. dollars increases.

12. **c.** Governments intervene in the foreign exchange market directly by buying or selling foreign currencies.

13. **b.** If the Fed switches to an easier monetary policy, the value of the dollar will drop as fears of inflation rise. Short-term U.S. interest rates will initially fall but will then rise as investors seek to protect themselves from anticipated inflation. Long-term rates will probably rise immediately because of fears of future inflation. Over time, however, if growth in the money

supply stimulates the economy to grow more rapidly than it would otherwise, the value of the dollar could rise, and so could real interest rates.

14. **c.** Since the Mexican peso devalued by 75% against the U.S. dollar, we have $e_1 = 0.25e_0$ $[(e_1 - e_0)/e_0 = -0.75]$. The appreciation of the U.S. dollar against the peso is 300% or

$$(e_0 - 0.25e_0)/0.25e_0 = 3.$$

15. **a.** Since the U.S. dollar appreciated by 500% against the cruzado, $e_0 = 6e_1$ $[(e_0 - e_1)/e_1 = 5]$. The devaluation of the cruzado against the U.S. dollar is 83.33% or

$$(e_1 - 6e_1)/6e_1 = -0.8333.$$

CHAPTER 3

THE INTERNATIONAL MONETARY SYSTEM

Overview

Exchange rate systems can be classified as free float, managed or dirty float, target zone, and fixed. The major difference between these systems is the degree of government intervention in the foreign exchange market. It ranges from no intervention in a freely floating rate system to full intervention in a fixed rate system. The current international monetary system can best be described as a hybrid system with some currencies freely floating, major currencies floating on a managed basis, and still other currencies moving in and out of various types of pegged currency relationships.

Many governments treat exchange rate policies as a secondary consideration to the more important domestic policy issues. As a result, exchange rates, whether fixed or floating, do not remain at their levels for long periods of time. In fact, the current system is often criticized for its rather volatile exchange rate movements. Thus, it is not surprising that both scholars and politicians frequently advance proposals to modify the system. The principal alternative to the current system of floating exchange rates is a fixed rate system. Unfortunately, past experience does not provide a convincing model which can be used to construct such a system.

Outline

I. The international monetary system represents the official part of the international financial system. It operates under a set of policies, institutions, practices, regulations, and mechanisms which determine the price at which one currency is exchanged for another.

   A. In a freely floating exchange rate system, exchange rates are determined solely by the forces of supply and demand which, in turn, are influenced by fundamental economic variables.

   B. In a system of managed exchange rates, also called a managed or dirty float, governments intervene in the foreign exchange market to smooth out exchange rate fluctuations. Exchange rates are also managed to establish unofficial boundaries within which exchange rates are allowed to move and to insulate the value of a currency against temporary disturbances.

   C. Under a target-zone arrangement, a central exchange rate is established with a specific margin around this rate. Member countries will adjust their national economic policies to maintain their exchange rates within that band. This exchange rate system is similar to the European Monetary System (EMS) which exists for the major European currencies.

   D. In a fixed rate system, governments are committed to holding the exchange rate constant or allowing it to fluctuate only within very narrow bands. If the exchange rate moves by more than the agreed-upon percentage, each central bank will intervene in the foreign exchange market to return the exchange rate to its par value.

E. Under the Bretton Woods system, which was in place between 1944 and 1971, exchange rates were fixed as in a fixed rate system. During this era, governments altered their currencies to correct persistent balance of payments deficits and surpluses. Policy alternatives to currency devaluation or revaluation include foreign borrowing, austerity, wage and price controls, and exchange controls.

F. The current system of exchange rate determination is a hybrid system with some currencies freely floating, major currencies floating on a managed basis, and still other currencies moving in and out of various types of pegged exchange rate relationships.

II. **During the past century, the world has experienced several international monetary systems.**

A. Between 1821 and 1914, most major currencies were on a gold standard.
1. Since gold is the dominant international money, each currency is valued in terms of a gold equivalent.
2. High production costs limit any short-run changes in the stock of gold.
3. Domestic prices are fairly stable, since the value of gold relative to other goods and services does not change much over long periods of time.
4. Balance of payments adjustments are automatic as prices across countries are equalized.
5. The period during which the classical gold standard prevailed was characterized by rapid development of international trade, stable exchange rates and prices, free flow of labor and capital across borders, rapid economic growth, and world peace.

B. The gold exchange standard was briefly in existence from 1925-1931. Under this standard, only the United States and Great Britain could hold gold reserves, while other nations could hold both gold and dollars or pounds as reserves.

C. The Bretton Woods system returned the world to a gold standard in 1944.
1. Each country agreed to maintain a fixed, or pegged, exchange rate for its currency in terms of gold or the dollar.
2. The U.S. dollar was the key currency in the system, and the value of $1.00 was set equal to 1/35 ounce of gold.
3. Since every currency had a defined gold value, all currencies were linked in a system of fixed exchange rates.
4. Exchange rates were allowed to fluctuate by 1% above and below their initially set rates.
5. Governments maintained the fixed exchange rates by buying and selling currencies in the foreign exchange market.
6. Periodic foreign exchange crises arose when governments failed to adjust currency values or make necessary economic adjustments.
7. The Bretton Woods system broke down in 1971 when the inflation rate in the United States began to rise and some countries refused to share the inflation experience imposed by the U.S. dollar.
8. The conference also provided for the establishment of institutions for aiding countries in their balance of payments and exchange rate policies--the International Monetary Fund (IMF)--and in general economic development--the World Bank. A third key institution is the Bank for International Settlements (BIS), which is the central bank for the industrial countries' central banks.

D. The years following the end of the Bretton Woods system were marked by the ups and downs of the U.S. dollar which was caused primarily by the changes in U.S. economic policy.
  1. In December 1971, under the Smithsonian agreement, the foreign exchange values of the major currencies were realigned. The U.S. dollar was devalued by about 8% which changed the dollar per gold exchange value from $35.00 to $38.02 per ounce of gold.
  2. The oil price crisis of 1973-1974 brought with it turmoil in the foreign exchange markets thereby removing any hope of returning to a fixed exchange rate system. It also caused the non-oil less developed countries to run balance of payments deficits.
  3. With the falling value of the U.S. dollar during 1977-1978, nations lost confidence in the U.S. currency which caused further instability in the foreign exchange markets.
  4. Between 1980 and 1985, the dollar strengthened substantially as President Reagan brought inflation under control.
  5. The dollar reached its peak in March 1985 and then began to fall which was caused primarily by a slowdown in U.S. economic growth relative to the growth in the rest of the world.
  6. By September 1985, the value of the dollar had declined by about 15%. But this decline was not considered adequate to help the growing U.S. trade deficit.
  7. With the Plaza Agreement in September 1985, the Group of Five designed a coordinated program which would force down the dollar further against other major currencies.
  8. This policy worked so well that another meeting was called in early 1987, known as the Louvre Accord, at which the Group of Seven agreed to support the falling dollar by pegging exchange rates within a narrow, undisclosed band.
  9. While the value of the dollar could be stabilized at a realistic and sustainable level in early 1988, it began to fall sharply in early 1990 thus continuing its ups and downs of the past 15 years.
  10. At the successful conclusion of the Persian Gulf war in spring 1991, confidence in the U.S. was restored which resulted in a strengthening of the U.S. dollar against the German mark and the Japanese yen. The dollar began falling again in 1993.

E. Since the advent of the floating rate system in 1973, real exchange rates have been rather volatile. While this instability can be partly attributed to disturbances in the world economy, it also reflects increased uncertainty over future government policies.

III. **The European Monetary System (EMS) is a target-zone arrangement which is maintained by the close coordination of macroeconomic policies of its member countries.**

A. The objective of the EMS is to provide exchange rate stability to all participating currencies which is achieved by holding exchange rates together within specified limits.

B. Member countries have their currencies tied to the European Currency Unit (ECU), a cocktail of European currencies with specified weights as the unit of account of the system.

C. Although the EMS helped to keep member currencies in a remarkably narrow zone of stability between 1987 and 1992, it has experienced its ups and downs.
  1. In the early years, the exchange rate system offered little anti-inflationary discipline which resulted in regular devaluations by Italy and France to offset higher inflation than that of West Germany.
  2. By January 1987, the values of member currencies were realigned 12 times despite heavy central bank intervention.

D. Foreign exchange market intervention failed to contain speculation because it was not supported by adjustments in national monetary policies. Thus, an EMS realignment became unavoidable.

E. In 1992, the EMS resorted to intervention in an attempt to maintain its increasingly misaligned exchange rates. But, once again, the system broke down in September 1992.
   1. The currency crisis ignited when the German Bundesbank decided to tighten monetary policy and force up German interest rates to fight inflationary pressures associated with the increasing cost of financing the German reunification.
   2. To defend their currency parities with the German mark, member countries had to raise their interest rates. They also intervened aggressively in the foreign exchange rate markets.
   3. With the rising cost of maintaining exchange rate stability, the market began to bet that some countries would devalue their currencies or withdraw from the exchange rate mechanism altogether.
   4. In fact, on September 14, 1992, Britain and Italy were forced to drop out of the ERM despite their costly efforts; Spain, Portugal, and Ireland devalued their currencies within the ERM; and Sweden, Norway, and Finland abandoned their currencies' unofficial links to the ERM.

F. During the summer of 1993, currency speculators tested the stability of the European Monetary System by attacking the weaker currencies within the ERM--particularly the French franc. Devastating speculative assaults on the ERM eventually forced the abandonment of the European exchange rate mechanism in August 1993.
   1. The adverse economic effects of the ERM during the fall of 1992 made it impossible for member countries to both lower interest rates and maintain their currencies within their ERM band unless Germany did so.
   2. When Germany refused to cut its discount rate on July 29, 1993, speculators began to doubt that weaker currency countries, such as France and Belgium, would be able to stay with the tight monetary policy of the Bundesbank.
   3. Currency speculators succeeded at great profit to themselves but heavy cost to the defending central banks.
   4. On August 1, 1993, the allowable deviation band within the ERM was adjusted to ±15% for all member currencies except the mark and guilder, which voluntarily maintain the old 2.25% fluctuation band. For the currencies of Spain and Portugal, the band was set at ±6%.
   5. Since the new trading bands are so wide, the European Monetary System has become a floating rate system.

G. The basic reason for the failure of the European Monetary System to provide currency stability is that member states have allowed political priorities to dominate exchange rate considerations.

H. Nonetheless, the EMS did achieve some significant success. By improving monetary policy coordination among member states, inflation differentials in Europe could be narrowed which, in turn, resulted in reduced exchange rate volatility until 1992.

I. The move towards monetary union by the European Community, as formalized in the Maastricht Treaty, would require the establishment of a single central bank with the sole power to issue a single European currency by 1999.

J. Adopting a common currency can help eliminate currency uncertainty and reduce the costs of currency conversion.

K. Maintaining separate currencies brings costs and benefits.
1. It is sometimes advantageous to simply change the value of a currency relative to another in response to various economic shocks.
2. But more currencies increase the costs of doing business and increase exchange rate risk.
3. Thus, maintaining more currencies would discourage international trade and investment, even as it insulates a country against economic shocks.
4. The theory of the optimum currency area states that this trade-off becomes less and less favorable as the economic unit reduces in size.

Fill-in-the-Blanks

1. The basic market mechanisms for establishing exchange rates include the _____ float, _____ float, _____-____ _____, and _____-_____ system.

2. Under a free float, exchange rates are determined solely by the _____ forces of _____ and _____.

3. A system in which governments intervene in the foreign exchange market to reduce exchange rate uncertainty is called a _____ or _____ float.

4. A target-zone arrangement, such as the _____ _____ ____, allows participating currencies to fluctuate within a _____ band.

5. Under a ____-____ ____, governments are committed to maintaining target exchange rates by _____ or _____ foreign currencies.

6. Currency _____ or _____ can also be achieved by borrowing abroad, reducing government spending and increasing taxes, imposing wage and price controls, and exchange controls.

7. Under the ____ _____, currencies are defined in terms of a ____ equivalent.

8. According to the _____-_____-____ _____, prices are equalized across countries, and the international payments are brought into equilibrium automatically.

9. The _____ _____ ____, which returned the world to a gold standard, broke down because the U.S. government issued too many dollars.

10. The ups and downs of the U.S. dollar can be largely traced to _____ in U.S. _____ policy.

11. The ____ _____ called for a coordinated program which was designed to force down the U.S. dollar against other major currencies.

12. The outcome of the Louvre Accord was to slow down the _____ dollar by _____ exchange rates within a narrow, undisclosed range.

13. The current system of _____ _____ ____ is characterized by increased exchange rate volatility.

14. Members of the _____ _____ _____ have given political priorities to exchange rate considerations.

15. Foreign exchange market intervention not accommodated by adjustments in national _____ _____ has only a _____ influence on exchange rates.

16. The _____ _____ of September 1992 was caused by the _____ monetary policy pursued by the Bundesbank to battle _____ pressures associated with the high cost of German reunification.

17. The need for the European Community to move towards _____ _____ is formalized in the _____ _____.

18. Maintaining _____ currencies acts as a _____ to international trade and investment, even as it _____ a country's vulnerability to economic shocks.

19. According to the theory of the _____ _____ _____, this trade-off becomes _____ favorable as the size of the economic unit shrinks.

Conceptual Questions

20. Managed floats fall into which of the following categories of central bank intervention?
    a. Smoothing out daily fluctuations
    b. Leaning against the wind
    c. Unofficial pegging
    d. All of the above
    e. a and b only

21. The current exchange rate system can best be characterized as a
    a. free float.
    b. managed float.
    c. target-zone arrangement.
    d. fixed-rate system.
    e. hybrid system.

22. The rising dollar in the early 1980s can be attributed to
    a. high real interest rates in the U.S.
    b. improved investment prospects in the U.S.
    c. the growing U.S. budget deficit.
    d. all of the above.
    e. a and b only.

23. Under the gold standard
    a. price levels rose dramatically.
    b. price levels stayed constant over time.
    c. the long-run stability of the price level includes alternating periods of inflation and deflation.
    d. all of the above.
    e. none of the above.

Answers

1. free; managed; target-zone arrangement; fixed-rate

2. free; supply; demand

3. managed; dirty

4. European Monetary System; narrow

5. fixed-rate system; buying; selling

6. devaluation; revaluation

7. gold standard; gold

8. price-specie-flow mechanism

9. Bretton Woods system

10. changes; economic

11. Plaza Agreement

12. falling; pegging

13. floating exchange rates

14. European Monetary System

15. monetary policies; limited

16. currency crisis; tight; inflationary

17. monetary union; Maastricht Treaty

18. more; barrier; reduces

19. optimum currency area; less

20. **d.** Managed floats fall into the following three distinct categories of central bank intervention: smoothing out daily exchange rate fluctuations, leaning against the wind which is aimed at preventing short- and medium-term fluctuations, and unofficial pegging.

21. **e.** The current exchange rate system is a hybrid system with major currencies floating on a managed basis, some currencies freely floating, and other currencies moving in and out of various types of pegged exchange rate relationships.

22. **e.** The dollar rebounded significantly due to economic expansion in the U.S. and high real interest rates which together attracted foreign capital.

23. **c.** The gold standard ensures long-run stability of price levels through alternating inflation and deflation.

CHAPTER 4

THE BALANCE OF PAYMENTS AND INTERNATIONAL ECONOMIC LINKAGES

Overview

The balance of payments catalogs the flow of economic transactions between the residents of a given country and the residents of the rest of the world during a certain period of time. This accounting statement, which is similar to a flow of funds statement, is based on double-entry bookkeeping; that is, for every credit entry there must be an equal and offsetting debit entry. The balance of payments consists of three distinct accounts including the current account, capital account, and official reserves account. In addition, there are balance of payments measures, such as the basic balance, net liquidity balance, and official reserve transactions balance, that summarize information helpful to analysts and government officials.

The United States is currently running a current account deficit which can be linked to domestic spending and production. A set of basic macroeconomic accounting identities show how a country's domestic policies affect its international economic relations.

Outline

I. **The balance of payments is an accounting statement which measures all financial and economic transactions between domestic and foreign residents over a specified period of time.**

A. This accounting statement is based on a double-entry bookkeeping system.
1. Currency inflows are transactions that earn foreign exchange and are recorded as credits.
2. Currency outflows are transactions that expend foreign exchange and are recorded as debits.
3. Credits have a plus sign, while debits have a minus sign.

B. The balance of payments consists of three major accounts.
1. The current account records the net flow of goods, services, and unilateral transfers.
a. Exports of goods and services are treated as credits.
b. Imports of goods and services are retreated as debits.
c. Interest and dividends are treated as services, because they represent payment for the use of capital.
2. The capital account reflects public and private investment and lending activities.
a. Capital inflows appear as credits, because the nation is selling valuable assets to foreigners in return for cash.
b. Capital outflows appear as debits, because they represent purchases of valuable assets from foreigners.
c. Capital account transactions are classified as either portfolio, direct, or short-term investments.

3. The official reserves account measures changes in international reserves owned by the country's monetary authorities. It reflects a nation's surplus or deficit on its current- and capital-account transactions by netting reserve liabilities from reserve assets.
   a. International reserves consist of gold and convertible foreign exchange.
   b. An increase in any of these assets shows up as a debit item.
   c. A decrease in reserve assets shows up as a credit item.

C. Balance of payments measures can be constructed by combining balance of payment accounts.
   1. The basic balance consists of the balance on current account and long-term capital flows. It emphasizes the longer term trends in the balance of payments.
   2. The net liquidity balance or overall balance includes the basic balance plus nonliquid private short-term capital flows and errors and omissions. It measures the change in private domestic borrowing or lending which is required to keep payments in equilibrium without adjusting official reserves.
   3. The official reserve transactions balance shows the adjustment to be made in official reserves for the balance of payments to balance.

D. Since the balance of payments must balance, any differences which cannot be traced to any particular transaction are recorded into an account called statistical discrepancy.

II. A set of basic macroeconomic identities links domestic spending and production to current account and capital account balances.

A. A nation that produces more (less) than it spends will have a net capital outflow (inflow) which shows up as some combination of a capital-account deficit (surplus) and an increase (decrease) in the official reserves account.

$$\text{National income - National spending} = \text{Savings - Investment}$$

B. The balance on current account must be equal to the net capital outflow or net foreign investment.

$$\text{Savings - Investment} = \text{Exports - Imports}$$

   1. A nation that is running a current-account deficit saves less than it invests (e.g., the United States).
   2. A nation that is running a current-account surplus saves more than it invests (e.g., Japan)
   3. An economically healthy nation which offers good investment opportunities tends to run a current-account deficit.

C. The balance on current account is equal to the private savings-investment balance less the government budget deficit.

$$\text{Current account balance} = \text{Savings surplus - Government budget deficit}$$

   1. A nation that is running a current-account deficit is not saving enough to finance its private investments and government deficit.
   2. A nation that is running a current-account surplus is saving more than is needed to finance its private investments and government deficit.

III. The two commonly mentioned solutions to a current-account deficit include a currency devaluation and protectionism.

    A. One principal suggestion to a current-account deficit is to devalue a nation's currency and make domestic goods more competitive.
        1. U.S. experience has shown that a currency devaluation does not improve a trade deficit.
        2. One explanation to this occurrence is the J-curve effect. It states that a decline in the value of a currency will initially worsen the trade deficit before showing signs of improvement.
        3. Another explanation is that the strong dollar and the trade deficit both resulted from the willingness of foreigners to hold U.S. assets.

    B. Another response to a current-account deficit is the imposition of tariffs, quotas, or other forms of government restrictions on foreign imports. Trade barriers, however, will most likely reduce both imports and exports by the same amount, leaving the trade deficit unchanged.

    C. Two additional approaches can be used to eliminate a current-account deficit.
        1. Ending foreign ownership of domestic assets will eliminate capital inflows, since foreigners now export an equal amount to what they are willing to import.
        2. Stimulating savings behavior by changing tax regulations and tax rates will affect a nation's trade and capital flows.

    D. It is claimed that a current-account deficit leads to unemployment, because domestic consumers substitute foreign goods and services for domestic goods and services. The large U.S. trade deficit during the 1980s, however, did not appear to have harmed the U.S. economy and its domestic performance.

    E. In a world in which nations trade with one another, it must be realized that one country's exports are another's imports. Thus, it is impossible for everyone to be running a current-account surplus. In fact, historical evidence has shown that current-account surpluses are neither good nor bad.

    F. On the other hand, current-account deficits are not inherently bad either. Rather than being a problem, they may become a solution to differing savings propensities and investment opportunities in the United States and the rest of the world.

Fill-in-the-Blanks

1. The _____ __ _____ records all economic transactions between residents of the home country and residents of all other countries.

2. _____ are credits and show up with a plus sign, while _____ are debits and show up with a minus sign.

3. The _____ _____ consists of the trade balance and the balance of current account.

4. Capital-account transactions are classified as either _____, _____, or ____-____ investments.

5. Transactions of the government are recorded in the _____ _____ _____.

6. The _____ _____ focuses on transactions that are fundamental to the economic health of a currency.

7. A _____-_____ _____ arises when a nation spends more than it saves.

8. The U.S. trade deficit can be traced to its _____ _____ _____.

9. To cope with a current-account deficit, governments _____ their currencies or impose _____ _____.

10. According to the _-_____ _____, a nation's trade deficit will worsen first before it improves following a _____ _____.

11. One way to reduce the trade deficit is to stimulate _____.

12. Governments attempt to eliminate current-account deficits because they supposedly lead to _____.

13. Trade flows tend to adjust to national preferences for _____, _____, and _____.

Conceptual Questions

14. A country's capital account balance is expected to
    a. decrease if its home currency is expected to weaken, other things equal.
    b. increase if its home currency is expected to weaken, other things equal.
    c. increase if interest rates decrease in that country and increase in other countries.
    d. a and c.
    e. none of the above.

15. An increase in the use of quotas is expected to
    a. reduce the country's current account balance, if other governments do not retaliate.
    b. increase the country's current account balance, if other governments do not retaliate.
    c. have no impact on the country's current account balance unless other governments retaliate.
    d. increase the trade volume of a country with other countries.
    e. none of the above.

16. The sale of U.S. Treasury bonds by a Frenchman shows up as
    a. a credit on the capital account.
    b. a debit on the trade account.
    c. a credit on the official reserves account.
    d. a debit on the official reserves account.
    e. none of the above.

17. The change in private domestic borrowing or lending required to keep payments in balance without adjusting official reserves is called
    a. the net liquidity balance.
    b. the balance of payments.
    c. the balance on current account.
    d. the balance on capital account.
    e. none of the above.

18. Tourism shows up on the
    a. merchandise account.
    b. current account.
    c. capital account.
    d. a and c.
    e. none of the above.

19. The most likely way to reduce the Japanese trade surplus is to
    a. revalue the Japanese yen.
    b. impose quotas on imports from Japan.
    c. boost Japanese savings.
    d. boost Japanese consumption.
    e. all of the above.

20. An increase in the current-account deficit will place _____ pressure on the value of the home currency, other things equal.
    a. upward
    b. downward
    c. no
    d. upward or downward depending on the size of the deficit
    e. none of the above

Answers

1. balance of payments

2. Exports; imports

3. current account

4. portfolio; direct; short-term

5. official reserves account

6. basic balance

7. current-account deficit

8. federal budget deficit

9. devalue; trade barriers

10. J-curve theory; currency devaluation

11. savings

12. unemployment

13. consumption; savings; investment

14. **a.** If the home currency weakens, foreign investors will be less willing to invest in the country's securities, thereby decreasing the capital-account balance.

15. **b.** By setting a quota or imposing a maximum limit on what can be imported, imports will be reduced, and the current-account balance increased.

16. **e.** The sale of U.S. Treasury bonds takes place in France, not in the U.S. Thus, it does not affect the U.S. balance of payments.

17. **a.** The net liquidity balance is a measure of the change in private domestic borrowing and lending which is necessary to keep payments in equilibrium without having to adjust the official reserves account.

18. **b.** Tourism is regarded as a service and, therefore, reflected in the service account which is part of the current account.

19. **d.** The Japanese trade surplus is largely the result of its high savings rate. To reduce this surplus, Japanese consumption needs to be stimulated.

20. **b.** The current-account deficit becomes larger as domestic consumers buy more foreign goods and services. To pay for these imported goods and services, the supply of the home currency is increased, thereby placing downward pressure on the value of the home currency.

CHAPTER 5

THE FOREIGN EXCHANGE MARKET

Overview

The foreign exchange market is the place where money denominated in one currency is bought and sold with money denominated in another currency. The ability to transfer purchasing power between countries facilitates international trade and capital transactions. Currencies can be exchanged in the spot market for immediate delivery or in the forward market for future delivery. Spot and forward rates are expressed either in terms of the home currency per unit of foreign currency or in terms of the foreign currency per unit of home currency. The forward rate is also stated as a discount from or premium on the spot rate. A cross rate can be calculated from the rates of two currencies each quoted against the dollar and then expressed in terms of a third currency.

Outline

I. **The foreign exchange market is the mechanism by which one is able to trade one currency for another.**

   A. There are two levels at which the foreign currency market operates.
      1. At the wholesale level, major banks trade with one another.
      2. At the retail level, banks deal with their business customers.

   B. Currencies may be bought or sold in the following two markets.
      1. The spot market is the market in which currency transactions take place immediately, usually on the second following business day.
      2. The forward market is the market in which currency transactions take place at a specified future date.

   C. The foreign exchange market is similar to the OTC market in securities, whereby trading is done over the telephone or through telex. No centralized marketplace exists except for a few places in Europe.

   D. Foreign currency trading is generally done by telephone, telex, or the SWIFT system.

   E. The major participants in the foreign exchange market include large commercial banks, foreign exchange brokers, and commercial and central bank customers.

   F. Technology has standardized and increased the speed by which international funds are transferred.

G. Automated trading, however, threatens the oligopoly of information held by currency traders today.

H. The widespread use of computerized foreign currency trading systems increases the foreign exchange market's liquidity.

I. The foreign exchange market is the largest financial market in the world with an average foreign exchange trading volume in 1992 at over $1 trillion daily, or $250 trillion a year.

II. **In the spot market, currencies are traded for immediate delivery.**

A. In almost all major newspapers, up to four different quotes or prices of the currencies most actively traded are displayed. These include the spot price and the 30-day, 90-day, and 180-day forward prices.

B. Quotes which are used for trades among dealers in the interbank market are expressed in the following two ways.
   1. The amount of U.S. dollars it will take to exchange one unit of foreign currency is referred to as quoting a currency in American terms. For example, one German mark can be traded for $0.56, also stated as $0.56/DM.
   2. The amount of foreign currency it will take to exchange one unit of the U.S. dollar is referred to as quoting a currency in European terms. For example, one U.S. dollar can be traded for five French francs, also stated as FF5.00/$.
   3. With the exception of the British and Irish exchange rates, all currencies are expressed in European terms.

C. When dealing with nonbank customers, banks in most countries quote currencies in direct terms. That is, the price of a foreign currency is expressed in terms of the home currency. For example, in Germany the U.S. dollar would be quoted in German marks, while in France it would be quoted in French francs.

D. Exchange rates are quoted in indirect terms in Great Britain and in the U.S. for domestic purposes and for the Canadian dollar. For example, the value of the British pound is stated in terms of the foreign currency, such as the U.S. dollar, German mark, French franc, etc.

E. An exchange dealer will usually quote two numbers.
   1. The first rate is the bid price. It is the price at which the trader is buying a given currency.
   2. The second rate is the ask or offer price. It is the price at which the trader is selling a given currency.
   3. In practice, only the last two digits of the decimal of a currency are quoted by the dealer.
   4. The bid-ask spread is the difference between the bid and ask prices of a currency and represents a transactions cost. It is usually stated in terms of a percentage cost and computed as follows:

$$\% \text{ spread} = \frac{\text{Ask price - Bid price}}{\text{Ask price}} \times 100$$

   The bid-ask spread is the discount in the bid price as a percentage of the ask price.
   5. Widely traded and less volatile currencies have smaller bid-ask spreads.

F. The cross rate is the exchange rate between two non-U.S. dollar currencies. Since all currencies are quoted against the U.S. dollar, the cross rate can easily be computed. For example, if the German mark is quoted at $0.50, and the British pound is quoted at $1.80, then the cross rate per pound is DM3.60 or DM3.60/£ = (1/0.50) × (1.80).

G. Currency arbitrage exists when exchange rate quotes differ between money centers. In this case, someone can profit by buying currency in one market at the lower price and selling it in the other market at the higher price. However, ready access to information has reduced the opportunities for profitable currency arbitrage.

H. Bankers who act as marketmakers by taking positions in foreign currencies expose themselves to exchange rate risk.

I. Currency transactions are based on verbal agreements which are later supplemented by a contract note.

III. **In the forward market, foreign exchange transactions are delivered at a future date.**

A. A forward contract is an agreement between a bank and a customer to deliver a specified amount of one currency against another at a specified future date with the exchange rate fixed at the time the contract is entered into. These contracts can be used by companies with future currency transactions to reduce their exchange rate risk.

B. The major users of the forward market are the arbitrageurs, traders, hedgers, and speculators.

C. Forward rates can be stated in two ways.
   1. The actual rate or outright rate is usually quoted to commercial customers.
   2. The swap rate or forward differential is used by dealers in the interbank market. That is, the forward rate is quoted as a discount from or premium on the spot rate.
   3. A currency is said to be selling at a discount if the forward rate expressed in dollars is less than the spot rate.
   4. A currency is said to be selling at a premium if the forward rate expressed in dollars is greater than the spot rate.
   5. The discount or premium may be expressed as an annualized percentage deviation from the spot rate.

   Forward premium (+) or discount (-) annualized =

   $$\frac{\text{Forward rate - Spot rate}}{\text{Spot rate}} \times \frac{12}{n} \times 100$$

   where n is the number of months forward.
   6. For example, if the spot rate on the French franc is $0.20, and the 3-month forward rate is $0.19, then the French franc is at a 20% discount {[(0.19 - 0.20)/0.20] × (12/3) = -0.2)}.

D. If the premium or discount on forward quotes is given in terms of points, the outright rate can be found by (a) adding the points to the spot rate if the currency is trading at a forward premium, or (b) subtracting the points from the spot rate if the currency is trading at a forward discount.

E. Exchange traders know whether the quotes in points represent a premium or a discount from the spot rate.
   1. If the first forward quote (bid rate) is smaller than the second forward quote (offer rate), then the forward rate is at a premium and the points are added to the spot rate.
   2. If the first forward quote (bid rate) is larger than the second forward quote (offer rate), then the forward rate is at a discount and the points are subtracted from the spot rate.

F. The bid-ask spread in the forward market rises with exchange rate volatility and forward contract maturities.

G. Forward cross rates are calculated in the same way as spot cross rates.

H. The rates quoted in the forward market are normally for one, two, three, six, or twelve months' maturities. Forward contracts with delivery in more than one year can be arranged for the most actively traded currencies.

I. Banks try to discourage speculative transactions by customers.

Fill-in-the-Blanks

1. The _____ _____ _____ facilitates international trade and investment.

2. In the _____ _____, major banks trade with one another, while in the _____ _____, banks deal with their commercial customers.

3. Currencies are traded in the _____ _____ for immediate delivery and in the _____ _____ for future delivery.

4. When the number of U.S. dollars per unit of foreign currency is given, the exchange rate is expressed in _____ _____.

5. When the number of foreign currency units per U.S. dollar is given, the exchange rate is expressed in _____ _____.

6. A _____ quote states a certain quantity of a foreign currency in terms of the home currency.

7. An _____ quote states the value of the home currency in terms of the foreign currency.

8. Exchange rates are given in pairs where the first quote is the _____ _____ and the second quote is the _____ _____ _____ _____.

9. The difference between the bid price and the ask price is called the _____-_____ _____.

10. A _____ _____ can be calculated from the rates of two currencies quoted against the dollar and expressed in terms of a third currency.

11. If exchange rate inconsistencies exist in different money centers, exchange traders will take advantage of _____ _____ opportunities.

12. In a _____ _____ between a bank and a customer, the exchange rate is locked in on future currency transactions.

13. If the forward rate is greater than the spot rate, then a foreign currency is at a ____ ____; if the forward rate is lower than the spot rate, a foreign currency is at a ____ ____.

Conceptual Questions

14. The world's largest currency trading market is
    a. New York.
    b. Frankfurt.
    c. Tokyo.
    d. London.
    e. Zurich.

15. Foreign exchange dealers are not exposed to any risks in the foreign exchange market.
    a. True
    b. False

Problems

16. Suppose the following direct quotes are received for spot and 30-day French francs in New York: 0.1160-68 4-6. What is the outright 30-day forward rate for the French franc?
    a. 0.1156-62
    b. 0.1164-74
    c. 0.1166-72
    d. 0.1154-64
    e. none of the above

17. Assume that a bank's bid rate on Japanese yen is $0.0041 and its ask rate is $0.0043. Its bid-ask percentage spread is
    a. 4.99%.
    b. 4.88%.
    c. 4.65%.
    d. 4.43%.
    e. none of the above.

18. The German mark is quoted against the U.S. dollar at $0.35, and the French franc is quoted against the German mark at DM0.31. What is the value of the dollar in Paris?
    a. FF3.226/$
    b. FF1.129/$
    c. FF0.886/$
    d. FF9.217/$
    e. None of the above

19. Suppose the spot and 180-day forward rates for the German mark are $0.3310 and $0.3402, respectively. The German mark is said to be selling at a forward
    a. discount of 2.8%.
    b. premium of 2.8%.
    c. discount of 5.6%.
    d. premium of 5.6%.
    e. none of the above.

20. The spot rate of the French franc is $0.1080 and the 180-day forward rate is $0.1086. The swap rate is
    a. 0.0006.
    b. 0.
    c. -0.0006.
    d. 0.1086.
    e. none of the above.

21. Suppose the British pound is quoted in New York at $2.4110, the dollar is quoted in Paris at FF3.997, and the French franc is quoted in London at £0.1088. Arbitrage profits per £1,000,000 equal
    a. £1,048,480.
    b. 0.
    c. £48,480.
    d. £1,000,000.
    e. none of the above.

Answers and Solutions

1. foreign exchange market

2. wholesale market; retail market

3. spot market; forward market

4. American terms

5. European terms

6. direct

7. indirect

8. bid price; offer or ask price

9. bid-ask spread

10. cross rate

11. currency arbitrage

12. forward contract

13. forward premium; forward discount

14. **d.** The world's largest currency trading market is London with daily turnover in 1992 estimated at $303 billion.

15. **b.** Foreign exchange dealers must cope with exchange rate risk, because of the foreign currency positions they take. They also bear credit risk, since the counterparties to the trades they enter into may not honor their obligations.

16. **b.** Since the first forward quote is smaller than the second forward quote, the forward rate is at a premium, and the swap rate is added to the spot rate. Thus, the 30-day forward franc rates are $0.1164-74.

17. **c.** The percentage bid-ask spread is 4.65% or (0.0043 - 0.0041)/0.0043= 0.0465.

18. **d.** FF/$ = FF/DM × DM/$
           = (1/0.31) × (1/0.35)
           = 9.2165

19. **d.** The German mark is said to be selling at a premium of 5.56%. That is,

$$p = [(0.3402 - 0.3310)/0.3310] \times (360/180) = 0.0556$$

20. **a.** The forward franc is at a premium of 6 points which is calculated as follows:

$$\text{Swap rate} = 0.1086 - 0.1080 = 0.0006$$

21. **c.** If the trader begins with £1,000,000, he/she could (1) sell pounds in New York at $2.4110 to receive $2,411,000 (£1,000,00 × $2.4110); (2) sell these dollars in Paris at FF3.997 to receive FF9,636,767 ($2,411,000 × FF3.997); and (3) sell these francs in London at £0.1088 to receive £1,048,480 (FF9,636,767 × £0.1088). The arbitrage profit realized equals £48,480.

CHAPTER 6

CURRENCY FUTURES AND OPTIONS MARKETS

Overview

Currency futures and currency options are derivatives whose value is derived from their underlying asset. These financial instruments can be used by individuals and companies for hedging and speculative purposes. Futures contracts are similar to forward contracts in that they must be settled at maturity. Currency options, however, give the holder the right, but not the obligation, to buy (call option) or sell (put option) a given amount of foreign exchange. An American option can be exercised at any time up to the expiration date; a European option can be exercised only on its expiration date.

Futures contracts are standardized contracts which are traded on organized exchanges. Forward contracts are custom-tailored contracts whose terms and conditions are negotiated between a bank and its customers. Option contracts can be bought on organized exchanges and in the over-the-counter market.

Outline

I. **Currency futures contracts, which are patterned much after grain and commodity contracts, are traded at the International Monetary Market (IMM) at the Chicago Mercantile Exchange (CME).**

   A. Currency futures are contracts which are written for a specific quantity of a given currency. The exchange rate is fixed at the time the contract is entered into, and the delivery date is set by the board of directors of the IMM.
      1. Futures contracts are currently traded in the British pound, Canadian dollar, German mark, Swiss franc, French franc, Japanese yen, and Australian dollar. Most recently, the IMM has introduced a cross-currency futures contract (DM/¥).
      2. Contract sizes are standardized for a particular currency. For example, a German mark contract is made for DM125,000. Fractions of a contract are not traded.
      3. The contracts also have minimum price changes.
      4. Transactions in the futures market require the payment of a commission to the trader rather than using the bid-ask spreads found in the forward market.

   B. Although forward contracts and futures contracts are similar, there are some major differences between them.
      1. Futures contracts are standardized contracts which are traded on organized exchanges; forward contracts are nonstandardized contracts made between a bank and its client.
      2. Futures contracts are marked to market daily; that is, at the end of each day, the contracts are settled and the resulting profits or losses paid.
      3. Market participants in the futures market are required to maintain a margin or security deposit with a broker.

4. Futures contracts are most useful for speculators and commercial customers who have stable and continuous cash inflows and outflows in foreign currencies.

C. Arbitrage between the futures market and the forward market ensures that futures rates will stay in line with forward rates.

II. **Currency options, which are now one of the fastest growing segments of the global foreign exchange market, were first traded at the Philadelphia Stock Exchange.**

    A. Currency options give the holder the right, but not the obligation, to buy or sell a given amount of a particular currency at a fixed price per unit for a specified time period.
      1. A call option is an option to buy foreign currency; a put option is an option to sell foreign currency.
      2. An American option gives the holder the right to exercise the option at any time up to the expiration date; a European option gives the holder the right to exercise the option only on its expiration date.
      3. An option that is in-the-money is profitable when exercised immediately; an option that is out-of-the-money is not profitable when exercised immediately.
      4. The exercise price or strike price is the price at which the owner can buy or sell the contracted currency.
      5. An option is at-the-money, when the exercise price equals the spot exchange rate.

    B. Currency options can be used by hedgers and by speculators.
      1. With a call option, the owner can profit (hedge) from (against) increases in the spot exchange rate.
      2. With a put option, the owner can profit (hedge) from (against) decreases in the spot exchange rate.
      3. Currency options are most appropriate when hedging currency transactions that are possible but not certain to occur.

    C. The theoretical value of an option consists of an intrinsic value and a time value.
      1. The intrinsic value is the amount by which the option is in-the-money; that is, $S - E$.
      2. The time value is the amount by which the option value is in excess over the intrinsic value.
      3. The value of an option rises with longer time to expiration and greater variability in the exchange rate.

    D. The valuation of foreign currency options is complicated by having to use both domestic and foreign interest rates.

    E. Option pricing is based on riskless arbitrage opportunities and a number of simplifying assumptions.

    F. Forward or futures contracts are more suitable than options when hedging a known future foreign currency cash inflow or outflow.

    G. Currency options are traded both on organized exchanges and in the over-the-counter market (OTC).
      1. Exchange-traded currency options are standardized contracts with predetermined exercise prices, standard maturities, and fixed maturities.

2. Currency options traded on the PHLX are of the American- and European-style and are available in seven currencies, the ECU, and in cross-currencies. The standard contract sizes are half the size of the IMM futures contracts.
3. The OTC options market operates on two levels: a retail market and a wholesale market.
4. The OTC options are custom-tailored to the specific needs of the customer, just like forward contracts.
5. The option buyer can lose only the premium paid for the option, while the seller's potential loss is unlimited.

   H. Futures options are contracts which give the owner the right to buy (call) or sell (put) a standard IMM futures contract in the currency rather than the currency itself.

III. **The prices of currency futures and exchange-listed currency options are published daily in the financial press, such as the *Wall Street Journal*.**

Fill-in-the-Blanks

1. Currency futures and currency options offer alternative _____ instruments for companies and individuals.

2. A _____ _____ is a contract which specifies a standard amount of a particular currency to be exchanged at a specific expiration date for a set price.

3. Customers in the futures market are required to pay a _____, whereas customers in the interbank market pay a net price for a forward contract.

4. Profits and losses on a futures contract are paid over at the end of each trading day, a practice called _____ __ _____.

5. When commercial customers and speculators have _____ and _____ streams of expected foreign currency cash flows, then futures contracts should be used.

6. A _____ _____ is a contract which gives the holder the right, but not the _____, to buy (___) or sell (___) a stated amount of a particular currency at a set price and expiration date.

7. An ___-__-___-_____ option is worthless on its maturity date.

8. An option has both an _____ _____ and a ____ _____.

9. When valuing currency options, both the _____ and the _____ interest rates must be used.

10. The value of an option increases with contract _____ and increased currency _____.

11. _____ currency transactions are best hedged with a currency option.

12. An option whose underlying asset is a futures contract is called a _____ _____.

Conceptual Questions

13. The basic difference(s) between forward and futures contracts is (are) that
    a. forward contracts are custom tailored while futures contracts are standardized.
    b. forward contracts are negotiated with banks whereas futures contracts are traded on an organized exchange.
    c. forward contracts have no daily limits on price fluctuations whereas futures contracts have a daily limit on price fluctuations.
    d. all of the above
    e. none of the above

14. Currency futures contracts are currently available in the
    a. British pound.
    b. Canadian dollar.
    c. Australian dollar.
    d. German mark.
    e. all of the above.

15. You can speculate on a pound depreciation by
    a. selling pound futures and buying a pound call option.
    b. buying pound futures and a pound put option.
    c. selling pound futures and a pound put option.
    d. buying pound futures and a pound call option.
    e. none of the above.

16. Options traded in the interbank market are known as
    a. listed options.
    b. exchange-traded options.
    c. over-the-counter options.
    d. all of the above.
    e. a and b only.

Problems

17. Suppose the current spot rate for the German mark is $0.5925. The premium on a call option with an exercise price of $0.5675 is $0.0373. What is the intrinsic value of one DM62,500 call option?
    a. $2,331.25
    b. $1,562.50
    c. $950.00
    d. $768.75
    e. None of the above

18. Suppose the current spot rate for the DM is $0.5925. The call premium on a call option with an exercise price of $0.5675 is $0.0373. What is the time value of one DM62,500 call option?
    a. $2,331.25
    b. $1,562.50
    c. $950.00
    d. $768.75
    e. None of the above

19. Assume that a speculator purchases a put option on British pounds with a strike price of $1.50 for $0.05 per unit. (A pound option represents 12,500 units.) Assume that at the time of purchase the spot rate of the pound was $1.51 and continually rose to $1.62 by the expiration date. Given the information, what is the highest net profit possible for the speculator?
   a. $1,500
   b. $875
   c. -$1,250
   d. -$625
   e. None of the above

20. Suppose that the interbank forward bid for March 20 on Swiss francs is $0.7827 at the same time that the price of IMM Swiss franc futures for delivery on March 20 is $0.7795. How much of an arbitrage profit could a dealer earn per March Swiss franc futures contract of SFr125,000?
   a. $400
   b. $68
   c. $215
   d. $58
   e. None. There is no arbitrage opportunity.

Answers and Solutions

1. hedging

2. futures contract

3. commission

4. marking to market

5. stable; continuous

6. currency option; obligation; call; put

7. out-of-the-money

8. intrinsic value; time value

9. domestic; foreign

10. maturity; volatility

11. Contingent

12. futures option

13. **d.** Forward contracts are nonstandardized contracts between a bank and a customer, whereas futures are standardized contracts traded on organized exchanges. Futures prices are allowed to fluctuate only within established price limits; forward price fluctuations are not limited.

14. **e.** Futures contracts are available in nine currencies which include the British pound, Canadian dollar, Australian dollar, and German mark.

15. **e.** You can speculate on a pound depreciation by selling a pound futures and buying a pound put option.

16. **c.** Options which can be bought and sold in the interbank market are called over-the-counter options.

17. **b.** The intrinsic value of an option is found as S - E or ($0.5925 - $0.5675) × 62,500 = $1,562.50.

18. **d.** The time value of one DM62,500 call option is $768.75 which is calculated as follows:

$$S - E = \$0.5925 - \$0.5675 = \$0.025$$
$$(\$0.0373 - \$0.025) \times 62,500 = \$768.75.$$

19. **d.** The premium of the option is $625 ($0.05 × 12,500). Since the option will not be exercised, the net profit is -$625.

20. **a.** On the March Swiss franc futures contract, a dealer could earn $400 [($0.7827 - $0.7795) × 125,000).

CHAPTER 7

PARITY CONDITIONS IN INTERNATIONAL FINANCE AND CURRENCY FORECASTING

Overview

Based on the law of one price, five parity relationships have been developed which apply to spot rates and forward rates, inflation rates, and interest rates in different currencies. These are the purchasing power parity, the Fisher effect, the international Fisher effect, the interest rate parity, and the forward rate as an unbiased predictor of the future spot rate. Parity is achieved through arbitrage in the markets for traded goods and financial assets worldwide. Although these parity conditions are only approximations to reality, a number of factors can cause significant and prolonged deviations from parity. For example, exchange rate risk and inflation risk may lead to different real interest rates across countries.

Interest and forward differentials between currencies provide useful information about future exchange rates. In addition, a variety of forecasting models are used by analysts to help outperform the market. The techniques applied vary with respect to the particular exchange rate system in place. Forecasting exchange rates in a fixed rate system is primarily a function of being able to predict government actions. On the other hand, forecasting exchange rates in a floating rate system will be a function of one's ability to forecast fundamental economic variables. Empirical evidence, however, has shown that the foreign exchange rate market does not differ from any other financial market in terms of its susceptibility to profitable predictions.

Outline

I. **According to the law of one price, goods sell for the same price worldwide.**

   A. The basis for this theory is that if the exchange-adjusted price of an identical tradable commodity is not equal worldwide, arbitrage in goods will ensure eventual equality.

   B. Five key international parity relationships result from these arbitrage activities: purchasing power parity, Fisher effect, international Fisher effect, interest rate parity, and unbiased forward rates.

   C. These parity conditions are linked by
      1. the adjustment of the various rates and prices to inflation.
      2. the notion that money should have no effect on real variables.

   D. Inflation and home currency depreciation are jointly determined by the growth of domestic money supply relative to the growth of domestic money demand.

   E. International arbitrage enforces the law of one price.

II. Purchasing Power Parity states that spot exchange rates among currencies will change to the differential in inflation rates between countries.

A. According to the absolute version of purchasing power parity, price levels adjusted for exchange rates should be equal across countries. That is, one unit of home currency should have the same purchasing power worldwide.

B. The relative version of purchasing power parity says that the exchange rate of one currency against another will adjust to reflect changes in the price levels of the two countries.
   1. In mathematical terms, purchasing power parity can be summarized as follows:

$$\frac{e_t}{e_0} = \frac{\left(1+i_h\right)^t}{\left(1+i_f\right)^t}$$

For example, if the home currency experiences a 5% rate of inflation, and the foreign currency experiences a 2% rate of inflation, then the foreign currency will adjust by 2.94% [(1.05/1.02) - 1 = 0.0294]. In fact, the foreign currency is expected to appreciate by 2.94% in response to the higher rate of inflation of the home country relative to the foreign country.
   2. A more simplified but less precise relationship of purchasing power parity is shown as:

$$\frac{e_1 - e_0}{e_0} = i_h - i_f$$

That is, the percentage change in the foreign currency should be approximately equal to the inflation differential for that same time period. In the above example, the foreign currency should adjust by about 3% (5% - 2% = 3%).
   3. Thus, purchasing power parity says that the currency with the higher rate of inflation is expected to depreciate relative to the currency with the lower rate of inflation.

C. If exchange rates adjust to inflation differentials according to purchasing power parity, real exchange rates remain the same. Thus, the competitive position of domestic and foreign firms will be affected only if the real exchange rate changes.

D. A currency's real exchange rate is the quoted or nominal exchange rate adjusted for its country's inflation rate relative to the inflation rate in other countries. That is,

$$e_t' = e_t \frac{\left(1+i_f\right)^t}{\left(1+i_h\right)^t}$$

E. Purchasing power parity restated in terms of the monetary approach to exchange rate determination is useful to predict domestic and foreign inflation rates. It is based on the following simple monetary model:

$$\frac{M}{P} = \frac{y}{v}$$

F. Empirical evidence has indicated that purchasing power parity holds up well over the long run, but not so well over shorter time periods.   Yet, currencies appear to move toward their purchasing power parity predicted rates.
1. Explanations for the deviations from purchasing power parity can be found in sticky goods prices and a combination of differently constructed price indices, relative price changes, and nontraded goods and services.
2. However, a clear relationship exists between relative inflation rates and nominal exchange rates.

III. The Fisher effect states that nominal interest rates are a function of the real interest rate and a premium for inflation expectations.

A. Formally, the Fisher effect is represented as

$$r = a + i + ai$$

or can be approximated as

$$r = a + i.$$

For example, if the real required rate of return is 2%, and inflation is expected to be 5%, then the nominal interest rate will be about 7%.

B. In a world where investors can buy any interest-bearing securities, real rates of return should tend toward equality everywhere through arbitrage. Thus, with no government interference, nominal interest rates will vary by the difference in inflation expectations, as shown by the following simplified equation:

$$r_h - r_f = i_h - i_f.$$

C. Thus, according to the generalized version of the Fisher effect, countries with higher rates of inflation have higher interest rates than countries with lower rates of inflation.

D. Empirical evidence has shown that differences in nominal interest rates across countries are caused by differing inflation expectations.

E. Capital market integration has homogenized markets around the world which, in turn, is eroding most of the real interest rate differentials between similar domestic and offshore securities.

F. Real interest rates tend to be equalized between countries. However, currency risk and high political risk particularly in developing countries can result in differences between the expected real returns of developing and developed countries.

IV. The International Fisher effect states that the spot exchange rate of one currency against another will adjust to the interest rate differential between the two countries.

A. The international Fisher effect is derived by combining the purchasing power parity and the Fisher effect.

$$\frac{(1+r_h)^t}{(1+r_f)^t} = \frac{e_t}{e_0}$$

B. Fisher postulated that the differential in nominal interest rates between two countries should reflect the difference in the rate of inflation between the two countries, since the expected real rates of return are equal in the absence of government restrictions.

C. A simplified equation for the international Fisher effect is presented as follows:

$$r_h - r_f = \frac{e_1 - e_0}{e_0}$$

For example, if the one-year interest rate on the Swiss franc is 4% and on the U.S. dollar is 13%, then the Swiss franc should appreciate by about 9% (13% - 4% = 9%).

D. Thus, according to the international Fisher effect, the currency with the lower interest rate is expected to appreciate relative to the currency with the higher interest rate.

E. Financial market arbitrage ensures that the interest rate differential between any two countries is an unbiased predictor of the expected future change in the spot rate.

F. Empirical evidence has indicated that currencies with high interest rates tend to decline (depreciate) in value, while currencies with low interest rates tend to increase (appreciate) in value.

G. To what extent exchange rates are affected by changes in the nominal interest rate depends on whether the change is caused by changes in the real interest differential or by relative changes in inflationary expectations.

V. **Spot rates and forward rates generally move in the same direction due to differences in interest rates between two currencies.**

A. The theory of interest rate parity states that the forward rate differs from the spot rate by a sufficient amount to offset the interest rate differential between two currencies.
   1. In equilibrium, the forward differential will be approximately equal to the difference in the interest rates of two countries.
   2. The premium (discount) on the forward rate of the currency with the lower (higher) interest rate will equal the interest differential.
   3. Interest rate parity is simplified in an approximated form as follows:

$$r_h - r_f = \frac{f_1 - e_0}{e_0}$$

   4. For example, if the interest rate on the German mark is 13%, and the interest rate on the U.S. dollar is 15%, then the forward mark should be at a premium of approximately 2% (15% - 13%).
   5. If this relationship between the forward differential and the interest differential does not hold, there is an incentive to profit from covered interest arbitrage.

B. The interest parity relationship results from the arbitrage activities of profit-seeking speculators, specifically covered interest arbitrage.
   1. Covered interest arbitrage takes place when someone can profit from borrowing in one currency and investing in another with a cover in the forward market.
   2. As the amounts of funds being moved between two currencies increases, pressures will develop in the foreign exchange market and in the money markets.
   3. In equilibrium, the returns on a covered basis on the currencies of concern will be the same so that no more profits can be realized.
   4. In such a case, it is said that interest parity exists.
   5. This no-covered arbitrage condition is stated as follows:

$$\frac{(1+r_h)}{(1+r_f)} = \frac{f_1}{e_0}$$

C. For example, the spot Danish krona is selling for $0.1740, and the 3-month forward rate is selling for $0.1744. The 3-month interbank rate (annualized) for the U.S. dollar is 11.6% and for the Danish krona is 11.25%. Since interest rate parity does not hold, an annualized gain of 0.5967% can be realized by borrowing funds in the United States at 11.6% for 90 days, investing them in Denmark at 11.25% for 90 days, and covering the sale of the krona with a forward contract maturing in three months. Here are the steps which show whether a covered interest arbitrage opportunity exists and how an arbitrageur can profit from it.
   1. Rearrange the no-arbitrage condition to show that the gross returns from investing at home and abroad are equal:

$$(1 + r_h) = (1 + r_f)(f_1/e_0)$$

   2. Convert the annualized U.S. and Danish interest rates into 90-day rates; i.e., 2.9% (11.6%/4) and 2.8125% (11.25%/4), respectively.
   3. Substitute the interest rate and exchange rate data into the above equation.

$$(1.029000) = (1.028125)(0.1744/0.1740)$$
$$(1.029000) \neq (1.030489)$$

   4. A covered interest arbitrage opportunity exists, because the gross returns from investing in the United States and in Denmark are not the same.
   5. A profit is realized by (a) borrowing dollars in the United States for three months at 11.60% p.a., (b) converting the dollars into krona at the spot rate, (c) investing the krona in a Danish money market instrument for three months at 11.25% p.a., and (d) covering the transactions with a 3-month forward contract to sell krona forward at $0.1744. These transactions will result in a 0.5967% annualized gain [(1+0.001489)4 -1]

D. Interest rate parity among currencies holds only if interest rates are net of costs, such as taxes on interest payments to foreigners, exchange and/or capital controls, transactions costs, etc. Since financial markets are usually not completely free, deviations from interest rate parity do occur.

VI. **A relationship exists between the spot market and the forward market.**

A. If the forward rate is unbiased, then it should reflect the expected future spot rate at maturity.

B. The unbiased nature of the forward rate (UFR) is stated as

$$f_t = \bar{e}_t$$

C. Based on empirical evidence, forward rates tend to be unbiased, though inaccurate, predictors of future spot rates.

VII. Inflation risk is the risk that actual inflation differs from expected inflation.

A. Inflation is a determinant of interest rates. Thus, as inflation becomes highly variable, interest rates will be affected which, in turn, will impact bond prices.

B. The longer a bond's maturity, the larger the change in the bond price due to changes in inflation rates. Inflation risk presents a major problem for long-term, fixed-rate bonds.

C. Corporate borrowers responded to the increased inflation risk by issuing:
1. bonds with shorter maturities.
2. bonds with interest rates that are adjusted whenever the funds are rolled over, so-called floating rate bonds.
3. bonds with interest rates tied to the inflation rate called indexed bonds.

VIII. The put-call option interest rate parity shows that option prices are related to interest differentials and, by extension, to forward differentials.

A. According to the put-call parity condition, the difference between a long call and a short put is equal to the discounted difference between the forward or futures contract and the exercise price. This relationship is stated as follows:

$$C - P = (f_1 - E) / (1 + r_h).$$

B. If put-call parity does not hold, someone can profit from risk-free arbitrage opportunities.

IX. While the parity conditions can be used to forecast exchange rates, a variety of currency forecasting models is used by analysts trying to outguess the foreign exchange market.

A. Successful currency forecasting is most likely when governments refrain entirely from intervening in the foreign exchange market.

B. In a world of fixed exchange rates, the forecaster must focus on the authorities' ability to hold to their announced commitment to devalue or revalue its currency.

C. To successfully forecast floating exchange rates, forecasters can use either market-based forecasts or model-based forecasts, neither of which provides a guarantee for success.
1. Market-based forecasts are derived from market indicators, such as forward rates and interest rates.
   a. The current forward rate contains implicit information about exchange rate changes for one year.
   b. Interest rate differentials can be used to predict exchange rates beyond one year.

2. Model-based forecasts include fundamental analysis and technical analysis.
    a. Fundamental analysis relies on examining key macroeconomic variables and policies which most likely will affect currency movements. These include inflation rates, growth in national income, and changes in the money supply.
    b. Technical analysis involves use of historical price and volume data to forecast currency values. The two primary methods of technical forecasting include charting and trend analysis.

D. Currency forecasters will not be able to consistently earn profits in an efficient foreign exchange market.

E. In a controlled environment, interest and forward differentials offer little information about exchange rate changes. In this situation, the black-market rate can be used as an indicator of future changes in the controlled currency.

Fill-in-the-Blanks

1. According to the ____ __ ____ _____, the domestic price level is equal to the product of the domestic price of foreign currency and the foreign price level.

2. _____ _____ _____ ensure that purchasing power parity, the Fisher effect, the international Fisher effect, interest rate parity, and unbiased forward rates hold.

3. _____ ____ _____ states that the foreign exchange rate must change to reflect the inflation differential between two countries. Thus, the currency with the _____ inflation rate should _____ relative to the currency with the lower inflation rate.

4. Deviations from purchasing power parity cause changes in the _____ _____ _____.

5. The Fisher effect shows that the quoted interest rate consists of two components: the _____ _____ _____ and a premium for _____ _____.

6. Since real interest rates tend to be _____ across countries, the _____ ____ _____ should be approximately equal to the anticipated _____ ____ _____.

7. The Fisher effect applied on an international basis says that currencies with ____ interest rates should _____ relative to currencies with low interest rates.

8. With highly variable _____ ___, _____-____ _____ are more affected than short maturity bonds.

9. To reduce _____ ____, companies tend to rely on debt with shorter maturities, floating-rate bonds, and indexed bonds.

10. According to the theory of the _____ _____ _____, the forward rate should equal the expected future spot rate.

11. If _____ ____ _____ does not hold, a condition called _____ _____ _____ exists.

12. The ___-____ _____ relates the option price to the interest differential and also the forward differential.

13. In a _____-____ _____, the task of the currency forecaster is to predict the timing of a devaluation or revaluation.

14. _____ ____ and _____ ____ contain implicit information about exchange rate changes.

15. Currency forecasting models either rely on _____ _____ or _____ _____.

16. In an _____ market, forecasting is unlikely to be consistently profitable.

17. ____-_____ _____ ____ are useful predictors of exchange rate changes in a controlled environment.

Conceptual Questions

18. If purchasing power parity holds even in the short run, then
    a. real exchange rates should tend to increase over time.
    b. real exchange rates should tend to decrease over time.
    c. real exchange rates should be somewhat stable over time.
    d. quoted exchange rates should be somewhat stable over time.
    e. c and d.

19. According to the international Fisher effect, if investors in all countries require the same real rate of return, the difference in nominal interest rates is caused by
    a. exchange rate movements.
    b. inflation differentials.
    c. real interest rate differentials.
    d. none of the above.
    e. all of the above.

20. Currency forecasting is impossible in a world of managed exchange rates.
    a. True
    b. False

21. The spot rate on the Dutch guilder is $0.39, and the 180-day forward rate is $0.40. The difference between the spot rate and the forward rate implies that
    a. interest rates are higher in the United States than in the Netherlands.
    b. the guilder has increased relative to the dollar.
    c. the interest rates are higher in the Netherlands than in the United States.
    d. the guilder is expected to fall in value relative to the dollar.
    e. none of the above.

22. If it was determined that changes in the exchange rate were not related to historical exchange rate changes, then _____ will not be useful to speculate on future currency movements.
    a. market-based forecasts
    b. fundamental analysis
    c. technical analysis
    d. all of the above
    e. none of the above

23. If the expected inflation rate is 5%, and the real required rate of return is 6%, then the Fisher effect says that the nominal interest rate is exactly
    a. 1%.
    b. 11.3%.
    c. 11%.
    d. 6%.
    e. none of the above.

24. If inflation in the United States is projected at 5% annually for the next 5 years and at 12% annually in Italy for the same time period, and the lira/$ spot rate is currently at L2400, then the purchasing power parity estimate of the spot rate five years from now is
    a. 1738.
    b. 3314.
    c. 2560.
    d. 2250.
    e. none of the above.

25. Suppose three-year deposit rates on Eurodollars and Eurofrancs are 12% and 7%, respectively. If the currency spot rate for the Swiss franc is $0.3985, what is the spot rate implied by these interest rates for the franc three years from now?
    a. $0.4570
    b. $0.8720
    c. $0.3435
    d. $0.4171
    e. none of the above

26. Suppose the price indeces in Spain and the United States are at 117 and 105, respectively, by the end of the year. Both began the year at 100. If the beginning and ending exchange rates for the peseta are $0.1320 and $0.1125, respectively, then the change in the real value of the peseta during the year is
    a. 0%.
    b. -5.0%.
    c. 2.4%.
    d. -8.2%.
    e. none of the above.

27. The 90-day interest rates (annualized) in the United States and Japan are, respectively, 10% and 7%, while the direct spot quote for the yen in New York is $0.004300. At what 90-day forward rate would interest rate parity hold?
    a. 0.004430
    b. 0.004271
    c. 0.004332
    d. 0.004176
    e. None of the above

28. Suppose the current spot rate of the pound sterling is $1.30, and the 90-day forward rate is $1.28. The 3-month deposit rates in the United States and Great Britain are 3% and 4%, respectively. If you use covered interest arbitrage for a 90-day investment of $1,000,000 which you currently have, what will be the amount of U.S. dollars you will have after 90 days?
    a. $1,024,000
    b. $1,030,000
    c. $1,040,000
    d. $1,034,000
    e. None of the above

Answers and Solutions

1. law of one price

2. International arbitrage activities

3. Purchasing power parity; higher; depreciate

4. real exchange rate

5. real required return; expected inflation

6. equal; nominal interest differential; inflation rate differential

7. high; depreciate

8. inflation rates; longer-term bonds

9. inflation risk

10. unbiased forward rate

11. interest rate parity; covered interest arbitrage

12. put-call parity

13. fixed-rate system

14. Interest rates; forward rates

15. fundamental analysis; technical analysis

16. efficient

17. Black-market exchange rates

18. **c.** Deviations from purchasing power parity cause real exchange rates to change.

19. **b.** If the real rate of return is the same across countries, then differences in nominal interest rates are caused by differences in inflation rates between countries.

20. **b.** Under a managed float, governments intervene periodically in the foreign exchange market to realign exchange rates. Currency forecasting must focus on the governmental decision-making structure, because the decision to intervene is political.

21. **a.** Since the forward rate is higher than the spot rate, the forward Dutch guilder is at a premium. A country whose forward rate is at a premium has an interest rate lower than that in the United States.

22. **c.** If a price pattern cannot be identified from past price data, the market is said to be efficient. Thus, speculators will not be able to beat the market and realize abnormal profits.

23. **b.** The nominal interest rate is exactly 11.3% or

$$0.05 + 0.06 + (0.05 \times 0.06) = 0.113.$$

24. **b.** The expected lira/$ spot rate in five years is L3314 or

$$(1.12/1.05)5 \times 2,400 = 3314.$$

25. **a.** The expected spot rate for the Swiss franc three years from now is $0.4570 or

$$1.12/1.07)3 \times 0.3985 = \$0.4570.$$

26. **b.** The change in the real value of the peseta during the year was -5.0% or

$$(105/117) \times \$0.1320 = \$0.1185$$

$$(\$0.1125 - \$0.1185)/\$0.1185 = -0.0506.$$

27. **c.** The interest differential is 3% in favor of the U.S. (10% - 7% = 3%). For interest parity to hold, the interest differential must equal the forward differential. Thus,

$$0.03 = [(FR - 0.0043)/0.0043] \times (360/90)$$
$$FR = 0.004332$$

28. **a.** The amount of U.S. dollars after 90 days is $1,024,000.

   (1) Convert $1,000,000 to pounds at the spot rate of $1.30 to receive £769,231 (1,000,000/1.30).
   (2) Invest £769,231 in Britain at 4% for 90 days receiving £800,000 (£769,231 × 1.04).
   (3) Sell pounds forward at $1.28 to receive $1,024,000 (£800,000 × 1.28).

CHAPTER 8

MEASURING ACCOUNTING EXPOSURE

Overview

Multinational corporations with foreign affiliates are required to translate their foreign currency denominated assets/liabilities and revenues/expenses into their home currency for accounting purposes. Several translation methods are available, including the current/noncurrent method, the monetary/nonmonetary method, the temporal method, and the current rate method. The Financial Accounting Standards Board mandates U.S. multinationals to use either the temporal method or the current rate method.

Since exchange rates may change during the operating year, the translation of balance sheet and income statement accounts may result in exchange gains or losses. To measure the accounting exposure, assets and liabilities are identified as exposed or not exposed. The difference between exposed assets and exposed liabilities represents the translation exposure.

Outline

I. **The financial statements of a multinational corporation's foreign subsidiaries must be translated from the local currency to the home currency prior to consolidation with the parent's financial statements.**

   A. Currency translation gains or losses may be realized if the exchange rate at the end of the operating year differs from that at the beginning of the year.
      1. If assets and liabilities are translated at the current exchange rate, they are considered exposed.
      2. Those translated at the historical exchange rate, that is the rate used at the time the asset was acquired or the liability incurred, are considered not exposed.
      3. Translation exposure is simply the difference between exposed assets and exposed liabilities.

   B. Four translation methods are used by multinational corporations around the world.
      1. Under the current/noncurrent method, current assets and current liabilities are translated at the current rate. Noncurrent assets and noncurrent liabilities are translated at the historical rate. Income statement items are translated at the average exchange rate of the period. An exception are those revenues and expenses which are related to noncurrent assets and liabilities.
      2. Under the monetary/nonmonetary method, monetary balance sheet accounts (cash, accounts receivables and payables, long-term debt) are translated at the current rate. Nonmonetary accounts (inventory, fixed assets, long-term investments) are translated at the historical rate. The income statement is translated at the average exchange rate during the period. Those revenues and expense accounts related to nonmonetary balance sheet

accounts are translated at the same rate as the rate used for translating the accounts on the balance sheet.
3. The temporal method is similar to the monetary/nonmonetary method with the only difference that inventory may be translated at the current rate if valued at market.
4. Under the current rate method, all balance sheet and income statement accounts are translated at the current rate.

II. **FASB-8 established uniform rules which governed the translation of foreign-currency-denominated financial statements and transactions of U.S. parent companies.**

   A. FASB-8, which became effective on January 1, 1976, utilized the temporal method for translating balance sheets and income statements into U.S. dollars.

   B. Unrealized translation gains and losses were recorded within the income statement. Thus, net income was greatly affected by fluctuating exchange rates.

III. **Increased dissatisfaction with FASB-8 resulted in a new translation rule: FASB-52.**

   A. Based on FASB-52, foreign-currency-denominated assets and liabilities are translated into dollars at the current rate. Income statement items must be translated either at the rate in effect at the time the revenues and expenses were incurred or at a weighted average exchange rate for the period.

   B. Unrealized translation gains and losses are recorded in a separate equity account on the parent's balance sheet, thereby completely bypassing the income statement. This account is called the cumulative translation adjustment account.

   C. In addition, FASB-52 distinguishes for the first time between the functional currency and the reporting currency.
   1. The functional currency of a foreign subsidiary is the currency of the primary economic environment in which it operates. Most companies have chosen the local currency as the functional currency.
   2. The reporting currency of a foreign subsidiary is the currency in which the parent firm prepares its own financial statements. Thus, for example, the balance sheet and income statement of a French affiliate of a U.S.-based MNC must be restated in U.S. dollar terms for consolidation purposes.

   D. A country which has experienced cumulative inflation of 100% or more over a three year consecutive period is considered a hyperinflation country. In this case, the functional currency must be the U.S. dollar.

   E. Under FASB-52, transaction gains and losses which arise from the need to adjust assets and liabilities denominated in a currency other than the functional currency generally are recorded within the income statement, whereas translation gains and losses are not.

   F. If the functional currency is the dollar, then the subsidiary's financial statements in local currency must be remeasured in dollars using the temporal method, as prescribed by FASB-8.

IV. **Transaction exposure results from the possibility of exchange gains and losses of transactions which have already been entered into and are denominated in a** foreign currency. It is measured currency by currency and is equal to the difference between contractually-fixed future cash inflows and outflows in each currency.

V. **In terms of measuring exposure to exchange rate changes, a major difference exists between accounting practice and economic reality.**

   A. Accounting exposure is the result from restating foreign-currency-denominated financial statements into the home currency. These assets and liabilities reflect past decisions made by the firm.

   B. Economic exposure focuses on the impact of exchange rate changes on the value of the firm as measured by the present value of all expected future cash flows.

   C. The definition of exposure which is based on market values assumes that the financial goal of the firm is to maximize shareholder wealth.

VI. **The accounting approach to measuring exposure ignores the effects that exchange rate changes may have on expected future cash flows.**

   A. Since there is no relationship between the information from retrospective accounting techniques and a firm's actual operating results, companies should focus on the economic effects of exchange rate changes.

   B. Empirical evidence has shown that sophisticated investors are able to distinguish between window dressing of accounting data and economic reality. Moreover, in an efficient market, translation gains and losses are placed in proper perspective by investors, so that the stock price of the multinational corporation will not be affected.

Fill-in-the-Blanks

1. _____ _____ is defined as the change in the value of a firm's foreign-currency-denominated accounts due to changes in the exchange rate.

2. The value of _____ _____ will change with exchange rate changes, while the value of assets ___ _____ remains constant.

3. _____ _____ is measured as the difference between exposed assets and exposed liabilities.

4. The temporal method is a modified version of the _____ _____.

5. FASB-8 is based on the _____ _____, while FASB-52 is based on the _____ ____ _____.

6. Under the temporal method, translation gains and losses are funneled through the _____ _____.

7. The _____ _____ _____ account is a separate equity account in which translation gains and losses are recorded under FASB-52.

8. If a country is considered _____, the _____ _____ must be the dollar.

9. _____ _____ measures the extent to which foreign currency denominated transactions already entered into will be affected by currency changes.

10. Economic theory focuses on the impact of changes in the exchange rate on _____ _____ _____.

Conceptual Questions

11. The current standard for measuring translation exposure is
    a. the current/noncurrent method.
    b. the monetary/nonmonetary method.
    c. FASB-8.
    d. FASB-52.
    e. none of the above.

12. The functional currency of a Mexican subsidiary that both manufactures and sells most of its output in Mexico will
    a. always be the U.S. dollar.
    b. always be the Mexican peso.
    c. be the U.S. dollar unless Mexico has a high rate of inflation.
    d. be the Mexican peso unless Mexico has a high rate of inflation.
    e. be none of the above.

13. Economic exposure can affect
    a. MNCs only.
    b. purely domestic firms only.
    c. a and b.
    d. none of the above.

Problems

14. Suppose the English subsidiary of a U.S. firm had current assets of £1 million, fixed assets of £2 million and current liabilities of £1 million both at the beginning and the end of the year. There are no long-term liabilities. If the pound depreciated during that year from $1.50 to $1.30, the translation gain/loss to be included in the parent company's equity account according to FASB-52 is
    a. 0 since the current assets and current liabilities cancel.
    b. +$200,000.
    c. -$250,000.
    d. -$400,000.
    e. none of the above.

Answers and Solutions

1. Accounting exposure

2. exposed assets; not exposed

3. Translation exposure

4. monetary/nonmonetary method

5. temporal method; current rate method

6. income statement

7. cumulative translation adjustment

8. hyperinflationary; functional currency

9. Transaction exposure

10. future cash flows

11. **d**. FASB-52 which is based on the current rate method has been in effect since December 15, 1981.

12. **d**. Since the primary economic environment of the Mexican subsidiary is Mexico, the functional currency is the Mexican peso. If Mexico had a high rate of inflation, then the functional currency must be the dollar.

13. **c**. Both multinational corporations and purely domestic firms are affected by economic exposure.

14. **d**. The net result is a translation loss of $400,000 calculated as follows:

Under FASB-52, the English affiliate has net pound exposure equal to

Exposed assets		
Current assets	£1.0 million	
Fixed assets	2.0 million	
Total exposed assets		£3.0 million
Exposed liabilities		
Current liabilities	£1.0 million	
Total exposed liabilities		£1.0 million

Net exposed assets		£2.0 million

At the original exchange rate of $1.50, the value of this net exposure is $3.0 million (£2.0 × $1.50). By the end of the year, this net pound exposure is worth only $2.6 million (£2.0 × $1.30) resulting in a difference of $400,000.

CHAPTER 9

MANAGING ACCOUNTING EXPOSURE

Overview

Multinational corporations exposed to exchange rate risk use forward contracts, borrow locally, and adjust their pricing and credit policies. In an efficient market, expected currency changes cannot be hedged. In fact, empirical research has shown that the forward rate is an unbiased predictor of the expected future spot rate. And, according to the international Fisher effect, interest rate differentials should be offset by exchange rate changes. Thus, the firm is primarily concerned with protecting its position against those exchange rate changes which are unpredictable and, therefore, unexpected.

Outline

I. **Transaction exposure arises whenever a company is committed to a foreign-currency-denominated transaction which takes place in the future.**

   A. To protect future currency inflows and outflows from adverse movements in the exchange rate, the multinational corporation can enter into a foreign currency transaction which exactly offsets in whole or in part the cash flows of the transaction exposure. This action taken centers around the concept of hedging.

   B. Hedging operations by multinational corporations include contractual hedges, such as the forward market hedge, money market hedge, and options market hedge, and operating strategies, which include price adjustment clauses, risk shifting, exposure netting, and currency risk sharing.

   C. The forward market hedge consists of offsetting a receivable or payable denominated in a foreign currency with a forward contract to sell or buy that currency with the delivery date set so that it will coincide with the anticipated receipt or payment of the foreign currency.
   1. The true cost of a forward cover is an opportunity cost which depends on the future spot rate at the time the forward contract is settled which is shown as

$$\frac{f_1 - e_1}{e_0}.$$

   2. In an efficient market, the real cost of hedging with a forward contract is zero.
   3. For example, a U.S. firm has imported goods from Germany valued at DM5,000,000 and payable in 180 days. The company can enter into a 180-day forward contract to buy DM5,000,000 for dollars today. If the 180-day forward rate is DM2.5802/$, then in 180

days the U.S. firm will exchange $1,937,834 (DM5,000,000/2.5802) for DM5,000,000 to pay for the shipment.

D. The money market hedge consists of reversing a foreign currency receivable or payable by creating matching payables or receivables in the respective foreign currency through simultaneous borrowing and lending in the money markets.
   1. For example, if a U.S. firm is obligated to pay FF1,000,000 in three months, it could hedge the exchange rate risk by borrowing dollars now, converting the dollars into French franc at the spot rate, and investing the proceeds in French money market instruments for three months. The amount received from the investment upon maturity will be used to meet the FF1,000,000 commitment.
   2. The amount of the U.S. dollar loan depends on the current spot rate between the dollar and the French franc and on the interest rate on the investment in French money market instruments.
   3. The gain or loss on the money market hedge is simply the difference between the cost of repaying the dollar loan and the French franc value of the investment.

E. Multinational corporations engaged in international trade can select the currency by invoicing exports in a strong currency and imports in a weak currency. This strategy will result in shifting the exchange rate risk to the other side of the international transaction. Its success depends on the relative bargaining power of the two parties involved.

F. When making foreign sales on credit, the foreign currency price is converted to the dollar price by using the forward rate, not the spot rate. By following this rule, it is recognized that a dollar tomorrow is not the same as a dollar today. If a number of payments are received at different time intervals, the foreign currency price should be a weighted average of the forward rates with maturity dates that coincide with the payment dates.

G. Protecting against exchange rate changes can be achieved by carefully selecting currencies so as to minimize net exposure. With exposure netting, the multinational corporation chooses currencies that are not perfectly positively correlated. Thus, the exposure in one currency is offset by the exposure in the same or another currency.

H. Companies may agree to share the exchange risk on their contracts by incorporating a customized hedge contract into the underlying trade transactions. This typically involves a price adjustment clause whereby the base price is adjusted to reflect exchange rate changes.

I. Companies incur business transactions which are possible but not certain to occur. In this case, a forward contract is not suitable to hedge against exchange rate changes. Rather, the company should use an options contract which gives the holder the right, but not the obligation, to buy (call) or sell (put) a specified amount of a foreign currency at a specified price during a stipulated period of time.
   1. A call option is valuable when a company is waiting for the outcome of a bid which, for example, may involve the purchase of foreign assets.
   2. A put option is valuable when a company awaits the outcome of a lawsuit in a foreign court.
   3. In both cases, the company is uncertain as to the amount and timing of the foreign currency inflow and outflow.
   4. Another use of currency options is to hedge exposure to shifts in a competitor's currency.

J. The objective of hedging involves matching the risk-return profile of the hedging instruments with the currency position to be hedged. Thus, a forward contract is best used when foreign currency cash flows are known, while an options contract is more appropriate when foreign currency cash flows are uncertain.

K. At times it may be better not to hedge at all, since hedging can lock in a company's dollar cost which, in turn, may give the hedged company a competitive disadvantage and increase its risk.

II. **Translation exposure results from the need to translate foreign currency-denominated financial statements into U.S. dollar terms.**

A. The basic hedging strategy to reduce translation exposure involves decreasing soft currency assets (hard currency liabilities) and increasing soft currency liabilities (hard currency assets).

B. With funds adjustment, the multinational corporation changes either the amounts or the currencies of the planned cash flows of the parent and/or its affiliates.
1. Direct funds adjustment deals with working capital adjustments.
2. Indirect funds adjustment techniques include the use of transfer pricing and leading and lagging.

C. Forward contracts are the most popular hedging instruments to reduce a firm's translation exposure. Currency selection, transfer pricing, and exposure netting provide additional tools but are used less frequently due to constraints imposed on these techniques by foreign governments.

D. When selecting the most appropriate hedging mechanism, firms should adjust their fund flows whenever it is profitable to do so on a covered basis no matter what effect it will have on translation exposure.

III. **The hedging strategies chosen by a firm are largely a function of management's objectives.**

A. The basic objective of hedging is to eliminate or reduce the variability of the consolidated earnings of the multinational corporation as a result of the unexpected currency fluctuations.

B. The statement of objectives will include management's beliefs about how the financial markets work and its view on the acceptable cost of exposure management.

C. Hedging exchange rate risk costs money and should be evaluated as any other purchase of insurance.

D. By taking advantage of tax asymmetries and market imperfections, firms can lower their hedging costs.

E. An important aspect of exchange risk management is the degree of centralization of foreign exchange transactions and the responsibility for developing and implementing the hedging strategies. Maximum benefits are achieved by centralizing all three functions, which include policy-making, formulation, and implementation, at the parent level.

Fill-in-the-Blanks

1. _____ currency exposure involves offsetting a currency position with a foreign currency transaction so that any gains or losses from the position are exactly offset by a corresponding loss or gain on the currency hedge.

2. Protective measures to guard against _____ _____ include forward market hedges, money market hedges, currency options, and price adjustment clauses.

3. In a _____ _____ _____, a company fixes the price today for future foreign currency cash flows.

4. The real cost of hedging is an _____ ____.

5. A _____ _____ _____ involves simultaneous borrowing and lending activities in two different currencies.

6. Transaction risk can be eliminated by pricing all contracts in the ____ _____.

7. The _____ ____ should be used when converting the dollar price of foreign sales into the foreign currency price.

8. _____ _____ can best be accomplished when offsetting positions in the same currency.

9. When the amount and timing of a future currency cash flow is unknown, a multinational corporation can protect itself against exchange rate changes by using a _____ _____.

10. To hedge translation exposure, firms can use _____ _____, _____ _____, and _____ _____.

11. Hedging exchange rate risk can be _____ and, therefore, should be evaluated like any other insurance purchase.

12. _____ the exposure management functions will reduce the amount of hedging needed to achieve a given level of safety.

Conceptual Questions

13. Hedging cannot provide protection against expected changes in the exchange rate.
    a. True
    b. False

14. If you fear the dollar will rise against the Spanish peseta, with a resulting adverse change in the dollar value of the equity of your Spanish subsidiary, you can hedge by
    a. selling pesetas forward in the amount of net assets.
    b. buying pesetas forward in the amount of net assets.
    c. reducing the liabilities of the subsidiary.
    d. selling pesetas forward in the amount of total assets.
    e. none of the above.

15. Assume zero transaction costs. If the 90-day forward rate is an accurate predictor of the spot rate in 90 days, then the real cost of hedging payables will be
    a. positive.
    b. negative.
    c. positive if the forward rate is at a premium and negative if the forward rate is at a discount.
    d. zero.

16. On March 1, Bechtel submits a franc-denominated bid on a project in France. Bechtel will not know whether the bid was accepted until June 1. What is the most appropriate way for Bechtel to manage the exchange rate risk on this contract?
    a. Sell the franc amount of the bid forward for U.S. dollars.
    b. Buy French francs forward in the amount of the contract.
    c. Sell a call option on francs in the amount of the franc exposure.
    d. Buy a put option on francs in the amount of the franc exposure.
    e. None of the above.

17. The basic hedging strategy for reducing translation exposure involves
    a. reducing soft currency assets and hard currency liabilities.
    b. increasing soft currency liabilities and hard currency assets.
    c. a and b.
    d. none of the above.

18. Multinational firms can almost always reduce the foreign exchange rate risk faced by their foreign affiliates by borrowing in the local currency.
    a. True
    b. False

Problems

19. American Airlines hedges a £2.5 million receivable by selling pounds forward. If the spot rate is $1.73, and the 90-day forward rate is $1.7158, what is American's real cost of hedging?
    a. $142,000
    b. $35,500
    c. $8,875
    d. $33,176
    e. It is unknown at the time American Airlines enters into its hedge.

20. International Worldwide would like to execute a money market hedge to cover a ¥250,000,000 shipment from Japan of sound systems it will receive in six months. The annual yen interest rate is 4%, and the current exchange rate is ¥124. What is the cost of the money market hedge to International?
    a. $2,016,129
    b. $1,976,597
    c. $1,938,586
    d. None of the above

21. A French firm has contracted to buy parts from Japan worth ¥15 billion payable in three months. The firm has receivables for goods sold to a Japanese firm valued at ¥5 billion, also due in three months. The spot rate of the French franc against the Japanese yen is ¥27.00, and the 3-month forward rate is ¥26.65. The annual interest rates on the French franc and the Japanese yen are 13.2% and 8.0%, respectively. What is the cost of the forward cover if the firm executes the desired hedge in the forward market?

a. FF 187,617,260
b. FF 375,234,521
c. FF 562,851,782
d. FF 370,370,370
e. None of the above

22. If, instead, the hedge is executed in the money market, what is the cost of the cover of this money market hedge?
a. FF 363,108,206
b. FF 375,090,777
c. FF 342,935,528
d. FF 388,203,017
e. None of the above

23. What is the foreign exchange gain or loss of an unhedged position (compared to a hedged position in the forward market) if the spot exchange rate in three months is ¥26.50 per French franc?
a. FF 377,358,490
b. FF 375,234,521
c. FF 2,123,969
d. FF 375,090,777
e. None of the above

24. Suppose that the spot rate and the 90-day forward rate on the pound sterling are $1.35 and $1.30, respectively. Your company, wishing to avoid foreign exchange risk, sells £500,000 forward 90 days. If the spot rate remains the same 90 days hence, would your company have been better off not to sell the pound forward?
a. The firm would have gained $125,000.
b. The firm would have lost $115,000.
c. The firm would have been better off not selling pounds forward.
d. Cannot tell
e. None of the above

25. A foreign exchange trader assesses the French franc exchange rate three months hence as follows:

$0.11 with probability 0.25
$0.13 with probability 0.50
$0.15 with probability 0.25

The 90-day forward rate is $0.12. What action will a trader take if he/she is concerned solely with expected values?
a. Buy French franc forward against the dollar.
b. Sell French franc forward against the dollar.
c. Nothing.
d. Cannot tell.

Answers and Solutions

1. Hedging

2. transaction exposure

3. forward market hedge

4. opportunity cost

5. money market hedge

6. home currency

7. forward rate

8. Exposure netting

9. currency option

10. funds adjustment; forward contracts; exposure netting

11. costly

12. Centralizing

13. **a.** Since expected exchange rate changes are incorporated in the currency prices, firms can protect themselves only against unforeseen currency movements with hedging.

14. **a.** The equity account which is adversely affected by a change in the dollar value can be offset by selling pesetas forward in the amount of net assets.

15. **d.** If the forward rate is an unbiased predictor of the future spot rate, the market is efficient and the expected cost of a forward contract is zero.

16. **d.** The franc-denominated bid on a project in France represents a contingent transaction. To protect against adverse exchange rate movements, Bechtel should buy a put option on francs (giving it the right to sell) in the amount of the franc exposure.

17. **c.** Translation exposure can be reduced by decreasing soft currency assets or hard currency liabilities and increasing soft currency liabilities or hard currency assets.

18. **b.** Replacing hard currency borrowings with local currency loans works in the case of an anticipated local currency devaluation. But this strategy does not work when the local currency is expected to appreciate.

19. **e.** The real cost of hedging is computed as $(f_1 - e_1)/e_0$. Since we do not know what the future spot rate in 90 days is, the cost of hedging cannot be determined.

20. **b.** International should invest the present value of ¥250,000,000, or ¥250,000,000/1.02 = ¥245,098,039 = \$1,976,597 at today's exchange rate of ¥124. In six months, International can liquidate its investment, which by then will have grown to ¥250,000,000, and use the proceeds to pay off its supplier.

21. **b.** Since the firm has yen payables of ¥15 billion and yen receivables of ¥5 billion, it needs to cover only the net exposure of ¥10 billion. In the forward market, it will enter into a 3-month forward contract to buy Japanese yen for FF 375,234,521 (¥10 billion/¥26.65). In 90 days, the company will exchange FF 375,234,521 for ¥10 billion to pay for the parts.

22. **b.** With a money market hedge, the firm will need ¥9,803,921,569 (¥10billion/1.02) to be invested in Japan.   To do so, it will need to borrow FF 363,108,206 (¥9,803,921,569/27.00) today in France. In 90 days, the firm will repay the loan to the French banker in the amount of FF 375,090,777 (FF 363,108,206 × 1.033).

23. **c.** Without a hedge, the company will wait for 90 days and exchange an unknown amount of French franc (depending on the spot rate in 90 days) for ¥10billion to pay for the part. If the expected future spot rate in 90 days is ¥26.50, then FF 377,358,490 (¥10billion/¥26.50) are needed to pay for the parts. Compared to the forward cover, the unhedged position will cost the firm FF 2,123,969 (FF 377,358,490 - FF 375,234,521).

24. **c.** With a forward market hedge, £500,000 are sold forward in 90 days. In three months, the company will receive $650,000 (£500,000 × $1.30). Without a hedge, the company will wait for 90 days and receive an unknown amount of dollars, depending on the spot rate in 90 days, of £500,000. If the spot rate remains the same 90 days hence, the company will receive $675,000 (£500,000 × 1.35). In this case, the firm should not have sold pounds forward.

25. **a.** The expected future spot exchange rate is $0.13 [($0.11)(0.25) + ($0.13)(0.50) + ($0.15)(0.25)]. Since the expected future spot exchange rate exceeds the forward rate of $0.12, the trader will buy French franc forward against the dollar.

CHAPTER 10

MEASURING ECONOMIC EXPOSURE

Overview

From an economic perspective, exposure focuses on the cash flow effects of exchange rate changes. This focus is largely ignored by the accounting profession, which is preoccupied with measuring and managing the balance sheet effect of currency changes. Moreover, the purchasing power parity shows that a close relationship exists between currency risk and inflation risk. Thus, for firms operating in numerous foreign countries, the net effect of currency appreciation and depreciation may be less important in the long run. Given the association between exchange rates and inflation rates, the inflation-adjusted, or real, exchange rate should be used when measuring economic exposure.

While exchange rate risk can be easily identified, measuring it in practice is much more difficult. The impact of exchange rate changes on the value of the firm depends on a number of variables, including the location of major markets and competitors, supply and demand elasticities, substitutability of inputs, and offsetting inflation. One technique used to determine the operating exposure of a firm is regression analysis.

Outline

I. **Economic exposure focuses on the impact of currency fluctuations on the value of the firm.**

    A. Expectations about exchange rate changes must be incorporated into all basic decisions of the firm. In order to do so, the firm must know what is at risk.
        1. The accountants emphasize the impact of currency fluctuations on a firm's balance sheet accounts.
        2. The economists emphasize the impact of currency fluctuations on future cash flows.

    B. Economic exposure is based on the extent to which the value of the firm, as measured by the present value of its future cash flows, is affected by changes in the exchange rate.

    C. Exchange rate risk then is the variability of a firm's value caused by unanticipated currency changes.

    D. Two components of economic exposure are transaction exposure and real operating exposure.
        1. Transaction exposure is the possibility of incurring exchange gains or losses on transactions already entered into and denominated in a foreign currency.
        2. Real operating exposure focuses on exchange rate changes combined with price level changes which could alter the magnitude and riskiness of a firm's operating cash flows.

E. The relative competitiveness of a company is affected only by changes in the real exchange rate.

F. If purchasing power parity holds, exchange rate changes will be exactly offset by the inflation differential between two countries. Thus, the real exchange rate will remain constant, and a firm's competitive position will not be affected by changes in the nominal exchange rate. In this case, the firm does not face real operating exposure.

G. Transactions fixed in foreign currency terms, however, will be exposed to currency fluctuations. If the real exchange rate is constant, the risk introduced is not exchange rate risk but inflation risk.

H. In general, an increase (decrease) in the real value of a nation's currency makes its exports and import-competing goods less (more) competitive.

II. **The true economic exposure of the multinational corporation is determined by the sector of the economy in which it operates, the sources of its inputs, and the changes in the real exchange rate.**

A. A transaction exposure report contains both on- and off-balance-sheet items.

B. A company's susceptibility to real exchange rate changes is determined by its degree of pricing flexibility and its ability to shift production and the sourcing of inputs among countries.
   1. Exchange risk is reduced (increased) for companies with highly (less) differentiated products, thus facing less (more) competition which, in turn, provides greater (lesser) pricing flexibility.
   2. Exchange risk is also reduced for companies that have greater flexibility in substituting between home-country and foreign-country inputs and production.

C. Domestic facilities which supply foreign markets incur much greater exchange rate risk than do foreign facilities that supply local markets.

III. **The following three examples help illustrate the identification of economic exposure.**

A. Aspen Skiing Company owns and operates ski resorts in Colorado. All its revenues and expenses are denominated in the U.S. dollar. Thus, its accounting exposure is zero. However, it faces exchange rate risk, because changes in the value of the dollar will affect its revenues while leaving expenses unaffected.

B. Petroleos Mexicanos (Pemex) is the largest oil company in Mexico with most of its sales made abroad. Since revenues are in dollars and expenses are in pesos, a change in the value of the dollar would affect its cost but not its revenues. For example, a peso devaluation would help Pemex.

C. Toyota Motor Company is the largest Japanese auto company with over half of its sales made overseas, primarily in the United States. Both its revenues and expenses will be affected by exchange rate changes. For example, if the yen appreciates, Toyota's yen revenues and yen costs will decline.

IV. The quantitative assessment of economic exposure depends critically on the underlying assumptions concerning the magnitude of future cash flows and their sensitivity to exchange rate changes.

V. Companies which take an economic approach to managing exposure need a proper measure of their economic exposure and the resulting exchange rate risk.

   A. Regression analysis can be used to determine a firm's economic exposure.

   B. Based on this approach, a company is exposed to exchange rate changes to the extent that variations in the dollar value of a unit's cash flows are correlated with variations in the nominal exchange rate. The following regression equation is stated:

$$CF_t = a + \beta\, EXCH_t + u_t.$$

   1. The foreign exchange beta coefficient measures the sensitivity of dollar cash flows to exchange rate changes.
   2. The larger (lower) the beta coefficient, the greater (lesser) is the impact of currency fluctuations on cash flows, and the more exchange rate risk the firm has.
   3. The reported t-statistics measure the statistical significance of the beta coefficient.
   4. The R^2 measures the fraction of cash flow variability which can be explained by variations in the exchange rate.
   5. In general, the higher the percentage of cash flow variability that can be explained by exchange rate changes, the greater the exchange rate risk a company has.

   C. A limitation of regression analysis to measuring economic exposure is the assumption that what happened in the past will happen in the future.

Fill-in-the-Blanks

1. _____ _____ is the possibility that the present value of the firm is altered by a given currency _____ or _____.

2. Accountants focus on the _____ _____ _____ of currency fluctuations, while economists focus on the _____ _____ _____ of exchange rate changes.

3. Economic exposure can be separated into _____ _____ and _____ _____ _____.

4. If the amounts and the riskiness of a firm's revenues and expenses are changed by the combined effect of currency fluctuations and changes in the price level, the firm faces _____ _____.

5. The competitive position of a multinational corporation is affected by only _____ _____ _____ _____.

6. If _____ _____ _____ holds, changes in the real exchange rate are _____. In this case, a firm is not exposed to _____ _____ _____ _____.

7. Transaction exposure can be eliminated by avoiding contracts _____ in foreign currency terms.

8. If the real value of a currency _____, the competitive position of domestic firms improves both at home and abroad.

9. The greater pricing flexibility of companies with _____ products _____ their exchange rate risk.

10. _____ _____ can help determine a company's economic exposure.

Conceptual Questions

11. The domestic counterpart of exchange risk is
    a. inflation risk.
    b. interest rate risk.
    c. relative price risk.
    d. all of the above.
    e. none of the above.

12. A U.S. firm selling exclusively in the United States and buying all its inputs from U.S. sources cannot be exposed to exchange risk.
    a. True
    b. False

13. During the year, the Spanish peseta depreciates from $0.09 to $0.084. At the same time, the price index at the end of the year is 112 in Spain and 105 in the United States (both started the year at 100). The net result of the peseta depreciation is that
    a. Spanish companies are now more competitive.
    b. American businesses in Spain have become less competitive.
    c. the competitive situation in Spain is unchanged.
    d. both a and b
    e. cannot tell

Problems

14. Suppose it costs DM 22,000 to build a Volkswagen in Germany, ship it to the United States, and earn a normal profit. During the year, the value of the German mark moved from $0.67 to $0.72. Ignoring inflation, what dollar price will Volkswagen have to charge at the end of the year to make as much as it did at the beginning of the year?
    a. $14,740
    b. $15,840
    c. $11,970
    d. $23,630
    e. None of the above

15. Suppose that a proposed foreign investment involves a plant whose entire output is to be exported. The plant's capacity is rated at one million units per annum. With a selling price of $10 per unit, yearly revenues from this investment equal $10 million. Since all sales are overseas, this revenue is not expected to vary with the local exchange rate. At the present rate of exchange, dollar costs of local production equal $5 per unit. A devaluation of 10% is expected to lower unit costs by $0.30, while a 15% devaluation will reduce these costs by an additional $0.15. Suppose that a devaluation of either 10% or 15% is likely with respective probabilities of 40% and 20%, respectively (the probability of no currency change is 40%). Depreciation at the current exchange rate equals $1,000,000 annually, while the local tax rate is 30%. What is the expected value of annual after-tax dollar cash flows given the above information and assuming no repatriation of profits to the United States?

a. $2.883 million
b. $3.947 million
c. $3.926 million
d. $3.275 million
e. None of the above

Answers and Solutions

1. Economic exposure; devaluation; revaluation

2. balance sheet effect; cash flow effect

3. transaction exposure; real operating exposure

4. operating exposure

5. real exchange rate changes

6. purchasing power parity; constant; real operating exchange risk

7. fixed

8. decreases

9. differentiated; decreases

10. Regression analysis

11. **a.** If real exchange rate changes are constant, and the nominal exchange rate changes, the risk introduced by entering into fixed contracts is not exchange risk but inflation risk.

12. **b.** Although both revenues and expenses are denominated in the U.S. dollar, a firm faces exchange risk, because changes in the dollar will affect its competitive position.

13. **c.** According to the purchasing power parity, the expected exchange rate should be $0.084 [(105/112) × $0.09 = $0.08437] which is exactly equal to the new exchange rate of $0.084. Thus, the competitive situation in Spain has not changed.

14. **b.** To keep profits unchanged, the dollar price of a Volkswagen will be $15,840, which is computed as

$$DM\ 22,000 \times \$0.72 = \$15,840.$$

15. **c.** The expected value of annual after-tax dollar cash flows is $3.926 million or

$$E(CF) = 0.4\ (3.8) + 0.4\ (3.98) + 0.2\ (4.07)$$
$$= 3.926$$

which is based on the following cash flow statement:

Cash Flow Statement
(in millions of dollars)

Devaluation	0%	10%	15%
Probability	40%	40%	20%
Revenues	10.00	10.00	10.00
Variable cost	5.00	4.70	4.55
Depreciation	1.00	0.90	0.85
EBT	4.00	4.40	4.60
Tax (30%)	1.20	1.32	1.38
EAT	2.80	3.08	3.22
Depreciation	1.00	0.90	0.85
Cash flows	3.80	3.98	4.07

CHAPTER 11

MANAGING ECONOMIC EXPOSURE

Overview

Currency risk affects all parts of a company. Thus, it should not be the concern of financial managers alone. Operating managers should develop marketing and production strategies that will help maintain the profitability over the long run. In fact, effective exposure risk management is based on the firm's ability to incorporate exchange rate changes in the decision-making process. This, in turn, requires a coordinated exchange risk program among executives responsible for different aspects of exchange risk management.

Outline

I. **While a firm can easily quantify and deal with exposures based on projected foreign currency cash flows, operating exposure, which is long-term in nature, is harder to measure and cannot be hedged with financial hedging mechanisms.**

   A. If exchange rate changes are caused by relative price changes, a firm's competitive position is changed.

   B. A company can deal with its competitive exposure by adjusting its production process or its marketing mix. By making the necessary production and marketing revisions, management can either counterbalance the adverse effects of, or capitalize on, the opportunities offered by a currency depreciation or appreciation.

   C. Managing economic exposure has led multinational corporations to reassess their reporting and internal control systems to cope with unpredictable markets and exchange rates.
      1. A strategy designed to react to currency fluctuations is not adequate.
      2. Multinational corporations need proactive marketing and production strategies that can be pursued in response to anticipated or actual real exchange rate changes.
      3. The appropriate responses to a currency fluctuation depend largely on how long that change is expected to last.

II. **The task of the international marketing manager should be to identify the likely effects of exchange rate changes and then to act on them by altering the pricing and product policies of the firm.**

   A. Market selection and market segmentation provide two major strategic considerations within which a firm may adjust the marketing mix over time. However, in the short run, neither of these two strategic choices can be changed to reflect actual or anticipated exchange rate changes. Rather, a firm should pursue certain tactical strategies, such as adjusting pricing, and promotional and credit policies.

B. When developing a pricing strategy, the following two key issues must be considered.
   1. The firm must decide whether to focus on market share or profit margin when coping with exchange rate changes. For example, if the value of the home currency is expected to increase, an exporter will gain a competitive price advantage by increasing unit profitability (price skimming) or expanding market share (penetration pricing).
   2. A multinational corporation must also consider the frequency by which prices should be adjusted to shield their customers from currency fluctuations.

C. Similarly, the promotional strategy should incorporate explicitly anticipated exchange rate changes. A major issue in any marketing plan is the size of the promotional budget for advertising, personal selling, and merchandising.

D. The product strategy can be altered as a function of a firm's relative exposure in different markets. Exchange rate fluctuations may affect the timing of new product introduction, the product deletion and product line decisions, and product innovation.

III. **Although pricing and other marketing strategies can save a product from currency fluctuations, the production process is altered when exchange rates have moved so much that the competitive risks cannot be managed by marketing changes alone.**

A. Multinational corporations manage their competitive risks through global sourcing and shifting production location.
   1. A well-managed firm should be searching constantly for ways to substitute between domestic and imported inputs, which depends on the relative prices involved and the degree to which substitution is possible.
   2. As a firm increases its production capacity, it should consider the option of designing new facilities that provide greater flexibility in making substitutions among various sources of goods.
   3. With a worldwide production system, a multinational corporation can allocate its production among its several plants in line with changing costs. For example, if a nation's currency has devalued (revalued), production there should be increased (decreased).
   4. The advantages of a global portfolio of production facilities must be traded off against the potential loss of economies of scale.
   5. As an alternative to shifting production abroad, companies with a strong home currency can try to improve their productivity at home.

B. Unanticipated exchange rate changes can be built into corporate strategies by projecting future cash flows under alternative exchange rate scenarios.

C. A firm's competitive position is greatly improved by simply shortening the product cycle, thereby reducing its operating exposure.

IV. **A multinational corporation should structure its financing so that it has breathing room while the necessary strategic production and marketing adjustments are made.**

A. In an integrated exchange risk program, the role of the financial manager is fourfold:

1. Provide local operating managers with forecasts of inflation and exchange rates.
2. Identify and focus on competitive exposure.
3. Design the evaluation criteria so that operating managers are neither rewarded nor penalized for the effects of unanticipated exchange rate changes.
4. Estimate and hedge the operating exposure which remains after the necessary marketing and production adjustments have been made.

Fill-in-the-Blanks

1. A multinational corporation can manage its operating exposure by adjusting its _____ and _____ policies.

2. Only _____ _____ _____ _____ will affect the value of the firm.

3. The appropriate marketing and production responses to currency changes depend on the _____ __ _____ this change is expected to last.

4. An international marketing manager should focus on identifying the impacts of exchange rate changes and then coping with them by adjusting _____ and _____ policies.

5. _____ _____ and _____ _____ are two important parameters within which a company can alter its marketing mix over time.

6. In the event of a home currency depreciation, an exporter may use either _____ _____ or _____ _____ to gain a competitive price advantage in the world market.

7. A firm can protect customers from exchange rate changes by offering them prices which are _____ in their local currency for a certain period of time.

8. Currency movements may affect the _____ of new _____ _____.

9. If marketing changes alone do not help reduce competitive risk, companies use _____ _____ and _____ plant locations.

10. In response to strong foreign competition, U.S. firms began to increase their _____ and improve _____ _____ through employee motivation.

11. Multinational corporations can plan for unpredictable exchange rate changes by using _____ _____.

12. Competitive exposure is reduced by _____ the time it takes to introduce new and improved products in the marketplace.

13. The financial manager should structure the multinational corporation's _____ in such a way that a reduction in asset earnings due to currency changes is _____ by a reduction in its financial fixed costs.

Conceptual Questions

14. The appropriate response of a U.S. exporter to a dollar appreciation would be to
    a. raise the foreign currency price if the dollar appreciation was expected to be temporary and the cost of regaining market share was minimal.
    b. move some production offshore if the appreciation were expected to persist for an extended period of time.
    c. keep the foreign currency price constant if demand is quite elastic.
    d. do all of the above
    e. do none of the above

15. A United States exporter who anticipates an appreciation of the dollar should
    a. sell foreign currencies forward.
    b. borrow foreign currencies.
    c. scout out possible foreign production sites.
    d. consider raising dollar prices on exports.
    e. all of the above.

16. Nissan, the Japanese car manufacturer, exports a substantial fraction of its output to the United States. What financial measures would be suitable for Nissan to take to reduce its currency exposure?
    a. borrow only yen to finance its operations.
    b. borrow dollars to finance part of its operations.
    c. sell yen forward in the amount of its annual shipments to the United States.
    d. buy yen forward in the amount of its annual shipments to the United States.
    e. none of the above

Problems

17. Suppose Apple is selling Macintosh computers in Germany for DM 5,500 when the exchange rate is $0.68/DM. If the DM rises to $0.71, what price must Apple charge to maintain its dollar unit revenue?
    a. DM 5,147
    b. DM 6,361
    c. DM 5,743
    d. DM 5,268
    e. None of the above

18. McDonald's charges 25 pesetas for a hamburger in Madrid. Its costs are 18 pesetas per burger, and these costs are not expected to change with the exchange rate. If the peseta devalues from $0.107 to $0.096, what price will McDonald's have to charge for its burgers to maintain its dollar profit margin?
    a. 25.80 pesetas
    b. 27.86 pesetas
    c. 22.43 pesetas
    d. 24.56 pesetas
    e. None of the above

Answers and Solutions

1. marketing; production

2. real exchange rate changes

3. length of time

4. pricing; product

5. Market selection; market segmentation

6. price skimming; penetration pricing

7. fixed

8. timing; product introduction

9. global sourcing; shifting

10. productivity; product quality

11. scenario analysis

12. shortening

13. liabilities; offset

14. **d.** If the dollar is expected to appreciate, an exporter can deal with this exposure by raising the foreign currency price if the dollar appreciation is expected to last only for a short period of time and if the cost of regaining market share is minimal; moving some of its production abroad if the appreciation is expected to last for a longer period of time; or keeping the foreign currency price constant if the demand is very elastic.

15. **c.** A firm without foreign facilities that is exporting to a competitive market whose currency is expected to devalue due to an expected appreciation in the dollar may find that locating new plants overseas may help to maintain unit profitability.

16. **b.** A substantial portion of Nissan's revenues are denominated in U.S. dollars. By borrowing dollars to finance part of its operations, Nissan can offset changes in the U.S. dollar affecting its revenues with those affecting its liabilities denominated in dollars.

17. **d.** To maintain its dollar unit revenue, Apple must charge DM 5,268 for each Macintosh computer sold in Germany.

$$DM\ 5,500 \times \$0.68 = \$3,740$$
$$\$3,740/\$0.71 = DM\ 5,268.$$

18.   **a.** McDonald's must charge 25.80 pesetas for its burgers in order to maintain its dollar profit margin. That is,

$$\text{(Ptas. 25 - Ptas. 18)} \times \$0.107 = \$0.749$$
$$\$0.74/\$0.096 = \text{Ptas. 7.80}$$
$$\text{New price} = \text{Ptas. 18} + \text{Ptas. 7.80} = \text{Ptas. 25.80.}$$

CHAPTER 12

SHORT-TERM FINANCING

Overview

Short-term financing for the multinational corporation is complicated by a number of factors, including interest rates, anticipated exchange rate changes, tax rates, the availability of forward contracts, and economic exposure. In addition, the firm and its subsidiaries have access to funds from a wide variety of borrowing sources. For example, foreign affiliates can obtain financing either from their parent company or sister affiliates as well as from external financial markets. They can obtain bank loans from the local or domestic financial market; they can tap the commercial paper market or the Eurocurrency market for their short-term financing needs. Given the financing options available, the multinational corporation must develop policies for borrowing either from within or outside the corporation in the presence of exchange rate risk and differing tax rates and regulations.

Outline

I. **The short-term financing decision in an international context is affected by six key factors.**

   A. If the international Fisher effect holds, then the expected dollar cost of borrowing will be the same for all currencies. But if deviations do exist, a trade-off must be made between the expected borrowing cost, which will vary from currency to currency, and the exchange rate risk associated with each financing option.

   B. The exchange rate risk associated with borrowing in foreign currencies is related to the firm's exposure in those currencies.

   C. The greater a firm's degree of risk aversion, the higher the price it should be willing to pay to reduce its currency exposure.

   D. If interest rate parity holds and in the absence of taxes, covered borrowing costs among currencies will not differ. In this case, the currency denomination of a firm's debt is irrelevant. When governments impose or threaten to impose capital controls, covered after-tax borrowing costs will differ among different currencies. In this case, the firm must decide in which currency to borrow.

   E. Tax asymmetries give rise to differing borrowing costs between countries. Thus, when comparing various financing alternatives, the relative borrowing costs must be measured on an after-tax basis.

F. In the event of political risk, a multinational corporation will use local financing rather than external financing, since fewer assets are at risk.

II. **Short-term financing objectives involve a trade-off between expected cost and risk.**

   A. When minimizing expected costs, risk is ignored, in which case borrowing options are evaluated on an individual basis without considering the portfolio effect between financial cash flows and operating cash flows. If forward contracts are used, then the financing alternatives should be compared on a covered (riskless) basis.

   B. By minimizing risk without regard to cost, a firm would sell all its assets and invest the proceeds in government securities.

   C. Trading off expected cost and systematic risk allows a firm to ignore the portfolio effect between financial cash flows and operating cash flows. Contrary to the previous objective, however, it is consistent with shareholder preferences according to the capital asset pricing model.

   D. Trading off expected cost and total risk requires the firm to consider the covariances between operating and financing cash flows. This objective should be followed only when forward contracts are not available and when financial distress costs are high.

III. **Temporary current assets are typically financed with short-term sources of financing which include intercompany loans, local currency loans, Euronotes, and Euro-commercial papers.**

   A. An intercompany loan can be provided by the parent company or sister affiliates.
      1. Exchange controls and length of the loan period may limit the use of these loans.
      2. Interest rates are to be set as high as possible for the lender's government and as low as possible for the borrower's government.
      3. The cost of these loans will be a function of the lender's opportunity cost of funds, the interest rate set, tax rates and regulations, the currency of denomination of the loan, and expected currency changes over the life of the loan.

   B. Bank loans are the dominant form of short-term financing around the world.
      1. Short-term bank loans are self-liquidating and typically unsecured.
      2. A clean-up clause may require a firm not to incur any other debts to the bank for at least 30 days during the year.
      3. A term loan is a straight bank loan, often unsecured, which is made for a fixed period of time, usually 90 days.
      4. A line of credit is an informal agreement that permits the firm to borrow up to a stated maximum amount from the bank. This type of bank loan is normally good for one year and can be renewed through renegotiations every year.
      5. An overdraft is a line of credit against which drafts (checks) can be written up to a specified maximum amount. This arrangement can be extended and expanded year after year, thus providing a medium-term loan to the firm.
      6. A revolving credit agreement is a formal line of credit. The borrower will pay a commitment fee on the unused portion of the funds to compensate the bank for guaranteeing that the funds will be available. This fee is paid in addition to the regular interest charged on the amount borrowed.

7. Discounting is the preferred short-term financing method in many European countries. In this case, a trade bill accepted by a bank, also called banker's acceptance, is sold at a discount to another bank or a money market dealer.

8. The interest rate on bank loans will vary for different kinds of borrowers and all borrowers over time. Rates charged will depend on the customer's credit worthiness, the previous relationship with the bank, and the length of the loan. It will also reflect actual and anticipated economic conditions in the particular country. Interest rates on bank loans can be calculated in several different ways.

   a. Regular, or simple, interest is paid at maturity. The effective interest rate is calculated by dividing the annual interest paid by the amount of funds received or:

$$\frac{\text{Annual interest paid}}{\text{Funds received}}$$

   b. Discount interest is paid in advance. Thus, the amount of funds received is reduced by the amount of interest paid, and the effective interest rate will be higher than the stated interest rate. It is calculated as follows:

$$\frac{\text{Annual interest paid}}{\text{Amount borrowed - Annual interest paid}}$$

   c. A compensating balance also raises the effective interest rate. It is typically computed for a regular bank loan as shown:

$$\frac{\text{Annual interest paid}}{\text{Amount borrowed - Compensating balance}}$$

   d. If the loan is discounted and the bank requires a compensating balance, the effective interest cost is found as:

$$\frac{\text{Annual interest paid}}{\text{Amount borrowed - Annual interest paid - Compensating balance}}$$

C. Multinational corporations favor commercial paper as a short-term nonbank financing technique.

   1. Commercial paper is a short-term unsecured promissory note. It is sold to institutional investors and other corporations on a discounted basis. Only very large and financially sound companies are able to tap the commercial paper market.

   2. Maturities are fairly standard among countries, ranging from 20-25 days in the United States to over three months in the Netherlands.

   3. Interest costs are relatively low because companies can go into the market directly and SEC requirements do not apply.

   4. Noninterest costs related to using commercial paper include backup lines of credit, fees to commercial banks, and credit rating service fees.

D. Euronotes and Euro-commercial paper are two additional nonbank short-term financial instruments.

   1. Euronotes are unsecured short-term debt securities usually denominated in dollars and issued by corporations and governments.

2. Interest rates are adjusted whenever the note is rolled over, thereby providing intermediate-term financing.
3. Euronotes are also referred to as Euro-commercial paper, particularly when these notes are not underwritten.
4. Although similar, U.S. CPs and Euro-CPs differ in some important respects.
   a. The average maturity on Euro-CPs is about twice as long as on U.S. CPs.
   b. There is a secondary market for Euro-CPs, while U.S. CPs are held until maturity by the original investor.
   c. U.S. companies issuing Euro-CPs are of lesser quality than their counterparts in the U.S. commercial paper market.
   d. A smaller fraction of issuers in the Euro-commercial paper market are actually rated, a situation which is changing over time.
5. A major advantage of the Euro-CP market is flexibility allowing corporate borrowers to issue Euro-CPs in a wide range of currencies.
6. The multicurrency Euro-CP program makes it possible to take advantage of swap arbitrage opportunities.

IV. **A break-even analysis can be used to determine the financing costs in dollar terms for local currency loans which may then be compared with the costs of alternative financing instruments.**

A. In the absence of tax considerations and forward contracts, the effective financing rate for a local currency loan and a dollar loan are easily computed.
1. The dollar cost of a local currency loan is equal to the difference between the interest cost and the exchange gain or loss. This is shown in the following equation:

$$r_L (1 - d) - d$$

where d equals the expected local currency change which is defined as $(e_0 - e_1)/e_0$.
2. For example, suppose that a U.S. firm is given a one-year loan of SF1,000,000 at the quoted interest rate of 8%. When the firm receives the loan, it converts the Swiss francs into dollars to pay a supplier for materials. The exchange rate at that time is $0.50/SF, in which case the firm receives $500,000. One year later, the U.S. firm repays the loan of SF1,000,000 plus interest of SF80,000. The total amount of Swiss francs needed is equal to SF1,080,000. Assume the Swiss franc moved from $0.50 to $0.60 by the time the loan must be repaid. Now the firm will need to convert $648,000 to the necessary amount of francs for repaying the loan. The effective financing rate is 29.5% computed as $148,000/$500,000 or, with the above equation, it is

$$r_F = 0.08 (1 + 0.2) + 0.2$$
$$= 29.6\%.$$

Note, the change in the Swiss franc from $0.50 to $0.60 represents an appreciation of 20% [($0.50 - $0.60)/$0.50 = -0.20].
3. The cost of a home currency loan (dollar loan) is simply the annual interest rate charged on the loan. For example, the U.S. firm could have also borrowed funds in the United States for one year, let's say at 12%. Then the dollar cost of the home currency loan is 12%.
4. Break-even analysis can be used to determine the amount of currency change that will equate the cost of local currency financing with the cost of home currency (dollar) financing. In general, the break-even rate of currency change is found as follows:

$$d^* = \frac{r_L - r_H}{1 + r_L}$$

where d* is interpreted as the expected local currency devaluation if positive or revaluation if negative.

5. Given the above example, d* is -3.7% [(0.08 - 0.12)/1.08 = -0.037]. That is, the Swiss franc appreciation should equal 3.7% before it becomes less expensive to borrow dollars at 12% than Swiss francs at 8%.

6. The borrowing decision rule for this example is stated as follows:

   If d > 3.7%, borrow dollars.
   If d < 3.7%, borrow Swiss francs.

7. The general borrowing decision criteria for an expected devaluation is:

   If d < d*, borrow dollars.
   If d > d*, borrow the foreign currency.

and for an expected revaluation it is:

   If d > d*, borrow dollars.
   If d < d*, borrow the foreign currency.

B. When taxes are taken into consideration, the calculation of effective interest rates on local currency financing and home currency financing is more complex.

1. The after-tax dollar cost of a local currency loan is equal to the difference between the after-tax interest expense and the exchange gain or loss on the principal. This is stated in the following equation:

$$r_L (1 - d) (1 - t_a) - d.$$

2. Suppose that the U.S. firm has an affiliate in Switzerland which can borrow in the local currency at a quoted interest rate of 8%. If the affiliate's tax rate is 40%, then the after-tax dollar cost of borrowing is 25.76% or [0.08 (1.2) (0.6) + 0.2 = 0.2576].

3. Note, the exchange gain or loss is not affected by taxes from the affiliate because the same amount of local currency was borrowed and repaid.

4. The after-tax cost of a home currency (dollar) loan to a foreign affiliate is equal to the after-tax interest expense less the tax write-off associated with the dollar principal, or

$$r_H (1 - t_a) - dt_a.$$

5. The break-even rate of a currency appreciation or depreciation is found in the same manner as in the no-tax case because the tax rates cancel out. As a result, the break-even value of d is:

$$d^* = \frac{r_L - r_H}{1 + r_L}.$$

IV. While a firm will be concerned about the expected dollar profit of an overseas investment, it must also consider the impact of the financing choice on the project's exchange rate risk.

A. The operating profit on an investment is equal to the difference between dollar revenue and dollar cost,

$$\Pi = I(1+s)e_1 - Ie_0$$

with a standard deviation of

$$Ó(\Pi) = I(1+s)Ó(e_1).$$

B. The cost of dollar financing is

$$C_H = Ie_0 r_H$$

with a standard deviation of

$$Ó(C_H) = 0.$$

C. The dollar cost of local currency financing is

$$C_L = Ie_1(1+r_L) - Ie_0$$

with a standard deviation of

$$Ó(C_L) = I(1+r_L)Ó(e_1).$$

D. The net profit after the financing costs can be calculated for home currency financing and local currency financing as follows:
   1. If financing is done in the home currency, the net profit after financing costs is

$$\Pi_H = [(I(1+s)e_1 - Ie_0] - Ie_0 r_H = I[(1+s)e_1 - (1+r_H)e_0]$$

with a standard deviation of

$$Ó(\Pi_H) = I(1+s)(e_1).$$

   2. If financing is done in the local currency, the net profit after financing costs is

$$\Pi_L = [I(1+s)e_1 - Ie_0] - [I(1+r_L)e_1 - Ie_0] = I(s - r_L)e_1$$

with a standard deviation of

$$Ó(\Pi_L) = I(s - r_L)(e_1).$$

Fill-in-the-Blanks

1. Expected costs and risk of any financing decision are influenced by deviations from the _____ _____ _____, and _____ ____ _____, _____ ____ ____, ____ _____, _____, and _____ ____.

2. The financing objective of _____ _____ _____ completely ignores risk.

3. An _____ _____ can be arranged between the parent company and its affiliate or between affiliates.

4. Local currency financing takes the form of ____ ____, which are a _____ form of short-term financing around the world.

5. _____ involves selling a _____ _____ at a discount to a bank or a money market dealer.

6. The effective interest rate on a discount loan is _____ than on a simple interest loan.

7. Commercial paper is generally issued by _____ _____ on a _____ _____ to institutional investors and other corporations.

8. _____ are short-term notes sold _____ the country in whose _____ they are denominated.

9. With ____-____ _____, the amount of currency appreciation or depreciation can be determined by equating the costs of _____ _____ and ____ _____ financing.

10. The break-even value of a currency change ____ tax considerations is _____ to the same value as for the _____-___ scenario.

11. The _____ _____ of a firm will be affected by its _____ _____.

Conceptual Questions

12. The effective financing cost
    a. adjusts the nominal interest rate for inflation over the loan period.
    b. adjusts the nominal interest rate for the change in the spot exchange rate over the loan period.
    c. adjusts the nominal rate for a change in foreign interest rates over the loan period.
    d. adjusts the nominal rate for the forward discount or premium over the loan period.
    e. none of the above.

13. If interest rate parity holds, and transaction costs are zero, covered foreign financing will result in an effective borrowing rate that is
    a. less than the domestic interest rate.
    b. greater than the domestic interest rate.
    c. equal to the domestic interest rate.
    d. greater than the domestic interest rate if the forward rate exhibits a premium and less than the domestic interest rate if the forward rate exhibits a discount.
    e. none of the above.

14. A risk-averse firm would prefer to borrow _____ when the expected financing costs are similar in a foreign country as in the local country.
    a. locally
    b. in the foreign country
    c. either a or b
    d. part of the funds locally, and part from the foreign country

Problems

15. SCI borrows SF1.5 million from Credit Suisse for one year at 12%. Interest is prepaid, and the compensating balance requirement is 15%. What is the effective Swiss franc interest rate on SCI's loan?
    a. 14.52%
    b. 13.37%
    c. 16.44%
    d. 21.22%
    e. None of the above

16. Intell has the choice of borrowing dollars at 9.5% or yen at 7% for one year. The current exchange rate is ¥152/$. At what end-of-year exchange rate would the yen costs of these two loans be equal?
    a. ¥156.0
    b. ¥149.2
    c. ¥153.6
    d. ¥148.5
    e. None of the above

17. Ford's Mexican affiliate is trying to decide whether to borrow for one year dollars at 10% or pesos at 40%. The peso-dollar exchange rate is expected to move from 160 pesos to 208 pesos by the end of the year. What is the expected after-tax dollar cost of borrowing dollars for one year if the Mexican corporate tax rate is 53%?
    a. -1.83%
    b. -11.2%
    c. -7.53%
    d. 0.05%
    e. None of the above

18. What is Ford's expected after-tax dollar cost of borrowing pesos for one year?
    a. -15.56%
    b. -8.62%
    c. 17.86%
    d. 2.29%
    e. None of the above

19. At what exchange rate will the after-tax peso cost of borrowing dollars equal the after-tax peso cost of borrowing pesos?
    a. $0.0217
    b. $0.0181
    c. $0.0076
    d. $0.0049
    e. None of the above

20. Mitsubishi Bank is willing to lend Toys-R-Us yen for its expansion plans at 6% payable at maturity with a compensating balance requirement. If Toys-R-Us wants to keep its effective interest rate below 7.5%, what is the highest compensating balance requirement it can tolerate?
    a. 10%
    b. 15%
    c. 20%
    d. None of the above

Answers and Solutions

1. international Fisher effect; interest rate parity; exchange rate risk; risk aversion; taxes; political risk

2. minimizing expected cost

3. intercompany loan

4. bank loans; dominant

5. Discounting; banker's acceptance

6. higher

7. large corporations; discounted basis

8. Euronotes; outside; currency

9. break-even analysis; local currency; home currency

10. with; equal; before-tax

11. currency exposure; financing strategy

12. **b.** The effective dollar cost of a local currency loan is computed as the nominal interest rate adjusted for the currency appreciation or depreciation as shown by the exchange gain or loss on repaying the principal.

13. **c.** If interest rate parity holds, then the nominal interest differential equals the forward differential. In this case, covered after-tax costs will be the same among currencies.

14. **a.** A risk-averse firm is likely to be willing to pay a high price to reduce currency risk. Thus, when local currency borrowing costs are similar to home currency borrowing costs, the firm will prefer the home currency loan.

15. **c.** The effective Swiss franc interest rate on SCI's loan is 16.44% which is computed as follows:

    Annual interest = SF1,500,000 × 0.12 = SF180,000
    Compensating balance = SF1,500,000 × 0.15 = SF225,000

    Effective financing rate = SF180,000/(SF1,500,000 - SF180,000 - SF225,000)
    = 0.1644 or 16.44%

16. **d.** If the end-of-year exchange rate is ¥148.5, the yen costs of these two loans would be equal. This is calculated as follows:

$$(152)(1.07)(1/x) - 1 = 0.095$$
$$162.64/x = 1.095$$
$$x = 148.5$$

17. **c.** The expected after-tax dollar cost of borrowing dollars for one year is -7.53%, or

$$d = (208 - 160)/208 = 0.2308$$

After-tax cost of dollar loan $= (0.10)(1 - 0.53) - (0.2308)(0.53) = -0.0753$

18. **b.** The expected after-tax dollar cost of borrowing pesos for one year is -8.62%, or

$$(0.40)(1 - 0.2308)(1 - 0.53) - 0.2308 = -0.0862$$

19. **d.** If the exchange rate of the peso is $0.0049, the after-tax peso cost of borrowing dollars will equal the after-tax peso cost of borrowing pesos. This is computed as follows:

$$d^* = (0.10 - 0.40)/1.10 = -0.2727$$

This represents a 27.27% appreciation of the dollar or a dollar against peso exchange rate of 203.63 (160×1.2727). In dollar terms, the value of the peso is $0.0049 (1/203.63).

20. **c.** Toys-R-Us can tolerate a 20% compensating balance requirement, or

$$0.075 = 0.06/(1 - x)$$
$$x = 0.2$$

CHAPTER 13

FINANCING FOREIGN TRADE

Overview

Foreign trade represents a large portion of the international activities of most multinational corporations. Trade-related working capital requires heavy financing which can come from the private sector or the public sector. Financing through commercial banks involves numerous documents. A draft is a written order to pay. A letter of credit is a bank guarantee of payment provided that certain conditions are met. A bill of lading covers the the title to the goods and the actual shipment of the merchandise by a common carrier. Documents of lesser importance include the commercial and consular invoices and the insurance certificate. In addition, there are government-sponsored export financing programs and credit insurance programs. The number of these institutions and the services provided has increased steadily due to the growing importance of international trade. Thus, a multinational financial executive must be aware of these different financing sources as well as the documents involved in moving goods across borders.

Outline

I. **The various forms of payment in foreign trade impose different risks on the exporter.**

   A. Cash in advance minimizes the payment risk to the exporter, because payment is received either before shipping the goods or upon their arrival. Cash terms are used when the importer's country is politically unstable, the buyer's credit is doubtful, or goods are made to order.

   B. A letter of credit (L/C) provides the exporter with the greatest degree of safety. It represents a bank guarantee of payment provided certain specified conditions are met by the importer and the exporter.
      1. Advantages to the exporter include: (a) Elimination of credit risk; (b) reduced default risk; (c) greater certainty about payment requirements; (d) protection against pre-shipment risk; (e) source of financing.
      2. Advantages to the importer include: (a) Greater assurance that merchandise is shipped; (b) inspection of documents; (c) better credit terms and/or prices; (d) lower source of financing; (e) easy recovery of money from a bank than from the exporter if proper shipment is not made.
      3. A documentary L/C is used with a commercial transaction requiring invoices or other documents; a nondocumentary, or clean, L/C is used in other than commercial transactions.

4. A revocable L/C can be canceled at any time without prior notice to the beneficiary; an irrevocable L/C cannot be canceled or amended without the specific permission of all parties involved.

5. A confirmed L/C is a L/C issued by one bank and confirmed by another bank; an unconfirmed L/C obligates only the issuing bank to honor any drafts drawn in compliance.

6. A transferable L/C gives the beneficiary the right to instruct the bank to make payment to one or more secondary beneficiaries; an assignment transfers part or all of the payment to another party without the necessary documents.

C. A draft, also known as a bill of exchange, is an unconditional order to pay.
1. The draft is a negotiable and unconditional financial instrument.
2. The three parties involved in a draft are the drawer, the payee, and the drawee (importer's bank).
3. A sight draft is payable upon presentation of documents, while a time draft is payable at some specified future date called usance or tenor.
4. A time draft becomes a banker's acceptance if accepted by a bank, or a trade acceptance if accepted by a company.
5. A clean draft is not accompanied by any necessary documents; a documentary draft is accompanied by all required papers.

D. Under a consignment arrangement, the exporter (consignor) ships goods to the importer (consignee) while still retaining title to the merchandise until the importer has sold them to a third party. Because of the risks involved, this arrangement is normally used only with related companies.

E. Selling on open account involves shipping the goods first and then waiting for the importer to remit payment according to the agreed-upon terms. While this payment method offers greater flexibility and lower cost, it is subject to the risk of currency controls.

F. Collecting overdue accounts from foreign customers is very difficult and expensive.

II. **Commercial banks may require numerous documents when providing trade financing, such as the bill of lading, commercial and consular invoices, and an insurance certificate.**

A. The bill of lading (B/L) covers the actual shipment of the merchandise by a common carrier and serves as the title of the goods.
1. A negotiable B/L establishes control over the goods; it is most commonly used in international trade transactions.
2. A straight B/L is consigned directly to the importer or consignee; it is neither negotiable nor transferable.
3. An order B/L is consigned to the exporter who retains title to the goods until the B/L is endorsed.
4. An on-board B/L certifies that the merchandise has been actually placed on board the vessel; a received-for-shipment B/L simply acknowledges that goods have been received for shipment.
5. A clean B/L indicates that the merchandise was received in good condition; a foul B/L indicates that the goods were damaged or in poor condition when received.

B. A commercial invoice lists the merchandise shipped by quality, grade, price per unit, and total value. It also provides the names and addresses of the exporter and the importer, the number of packages, any noted marks, the payment terms, and any other expenses, such as transportation and insurance charges.

C. An insurance certificate contains information on the goods shipped and indicates that the shipment has been insured by the exporter.

D. A consular invoice, which provides information about the merchandise, is exchanged for a visa at the local consul.

III. **Several other methods of financing international trade are available, including bankers' acceptances, discounting, factoring and forfaiting.**

A. The banker's acceptance is a time draft drawn on and accepted by a bank which agrees to pay a stated amount at maturity.
   1. The creation of a banker's acceptance begins with the importer requesting its local bank to issue a L/C on its behalf. The L/C allows the exporter to draw a time draft on the bank in payment for the merchandise. The exporter presents the time draft and the endorsed shipping documents to its local bank which, in turn, forwards the draft and any accompanying documents to the importer's bank. When the importer's bank accepts the draft, the banker's acceptance is created.
   2. If the exporter does not want to wait for payment until the specified maturity date, it can request that the banker's acceptance be discounted. The proceeds from the sale of the banker's acceptance will be less than if the exporter would wait to receive payment at maturity.
   3. Acceptances created to finance domestic shipment and storage of goods represent a small part of the market.
   4. Bankers' acceptances have typical maturities of 30-, 90-, and 180-days, with the average being 90 days. Maturities can also be custom-tailored to cover the entire period needed to ship and dispose of the merchandise financed.
   5. Market yields on bankers' acceptances are similar to those on CDs.
   6. A fee of less than 1% per annum is charged by banks for accepting the draft.

B. A trade draft can be converted into cash by way of discounting.
   1. The exporter sells the trade draft to a bank or other financial institution and, in return, receives the face value of the draft less any interest and commissions.
   2. The discount rate for trade papers is typically lower than that for prime-based borrowings.
   3. Discounting may be done with or without recourse.

C. Firms with a substantial export business can sell their receivables at a discount to a factor for cash.
   1. If factoring is done on a nonrecourse basis, the factor assumes all credit and political risks except for those involving disputes between the parties involved in the transaction.
   2. If factoring is done on a recourse basis, the exporter assumes all these risks.
   3. Fees can range from 1.75% to 2% of sales.
   4. Although factoring can be quite expensive, it is most beneficial for the occasional exporter and the exporter with a geographically diverse portfolio of accounts receivables.
   5. Factors are often better able to asses and bear credit risk.

D. Forfaiting is a specialized factoring technique which involves discounting medium-term export receivables denominated in fully convertible currencies at a fixed rate without recourse.

1. This financing arrangement is used for capital-goods exports with a five-year maturity and repayment in semiannual installments.
2. The discount rate is set at a fixed rate, typically about 1.25% above the local borrowing rate or the London Interbank Offer Rate (LIBOR).

IV. Governments of most developed countries offer a number of export financing programs and credit insurance programs to the exporter as well as the importer.

    A. Low cost export financing is often provided by governments to boost their exports.
       1. The Export-Import Bank (Eximbank) is a U.S. government agency which finances and facilitates U.S. exports.
          a. The Eximbank provides fixed-rate financing for U.S. export sales facing competition from foreign export financing agencies.
          b. Programs offered include direct loans to foreign buyers of U.S. exports, intermediary loans to financial institutions extending loans to foreign buyers, loan guarantees, export-related working capital loans, and preliminary commitments.
          c. In addition to interest rates charged on Eximbank loans, there is a front-end exposure fee which is assessed at the time of loan disbursement.
          d. Eximbank terms depend on the risk of the transaction and the degree of competition from foreign export financing agencies.
          e. Foreign mixed-credit financing involves a combination of grants and low-cost interest loans which is tied to the acceptance of specific commercial contracts.
       2. The Private Export Funding Corporation (PEFCO) finances U.S. exports of big-ticket items from private sources.
          a. PEFCO purchases medium- to long-term loans from importers of U.S. products at fixed interest rates.
          b. Foreign importer loans are financed through the sale of PEFCO's own securities.
          c. The Eximbank provides guarantees of repayment on all of PEFCO's foreign obligations.

    B. Government export financing agencies are shifting to buyer credits and are acting as catalysts to attract private capital.

    C. Export financing offered by the Eximbank at below-market rates to help U.S. exporters leaves a persistent deficit, which must be paid by the U.S. taxpayers.

    D. The Foreign Credit Insurance Association (FCIA) offers a broad range of short-term and medium-term insurance policies to protect against losses from political and commercial risks.
       1. By having insurance protection, the exporter can obtain financing from a bank with the insured receivables serving as collateral.
       2. The exporter is also able to borrow funds from private institutions at low rates, thereby remaining competitive.
       3. For providing the insurance, the FCIA charges premiums based on the types of buyers, countries, and terms of payment.

V. In recent years, more and more multinational corporations have been confronted with countertrade opportunities, particularly in the Eastern European countries and the Third World countries.

    A. Countertrade involves foreign trade transactions in which the sale of goods to one country is linked to the purchase or exchange of goods from that same country.

    B. The different forms of countertrade include barter, counterpurchase, and buyback.

1. Barter is the direct exchange of goods between two parties without the use of any currency as the medium of exchange.
2. Counterpurchase or parallel barter is the exchange of goods which are unrelated to each other.
3. Buyback or compensation arrangement involves the repayment of the original purchase price through the sale of a related product.

C. Many multinational corporations involved in countertrade view it as a necessary evil.

D. Countertrading countries try to ensure that goods taken in countertrade will not cannibalize their existing cash exports.

Fill-in-the-Blanks

1. _____ ____ _____ require some kind of financing.

2. Different payment terms used in international trade impose different _____ on the exporter.

3. The exporter has _____ protection, if payment is made in _____ either before the goods are sent or upon their arrival.

4. A _____ __ _____ is issued by the bank on behalf of the importer guaranteeing to pay the exporter provided certain stipulated conditions are met.

5. The most important advantage of a L/C to the exporter is that it eliminates _____ _____.

6. The _____ L/C substitutes the bank's name for the importer's name.

7. A _____ L/C protects the exporter against any problems with the bank that issued the L/C.

8. The draft is an _____ written order to pay the face amount of the draft upon presentation (_____ ____) or at a specified future date (_____ ____).

9. Most drafts in international trade transactions are accompanied by _____ to be delivered to the _____ on payment or acceptance of the draft.

10. Merchandise shipped to the importer first and paid later is subject to the risk of _____ _____.

11. The bill of lading serves as a _____ for shipment, a _____ of freight charges, and most importantly, conveys _____ to the merchandise.

12. Trade documents of lesser importance include the _____ and _____ _____ and the _____ _____.

13. A banker's acceptance is a ____ __ _____, or _____ ____, drawn on and accepted by a bank.

14. An importer can finance its goods with a _____ _____ until the merchandise can be resold.

15. _____ is used to convert a trade draft into cash.

16. Governments often provide _____ export credits to boost exports.

17. The ____-____ ____ offers low-cost export financing programs and credit insurance programs.

18. Eximbank terms depend on the ____ of the transactions and the degree of _____ from foreign export financing agencies.

19. Subsidized government export credit insurance enables exporters to obtain financing from financial institutions at _____-market rates.

20. _____ involves the purchase or exchange of goods from the same country which purchased goods from a multinational corporation.

Conceptual Questions

21. Which of the following L/Cs is safest for the exporter?
    a. Revocable, confirmed L/C
    b. Irrevocable, unconfirmed L/C
    c. Irrevocable, confirmed L/C
    d. Revocable L/C
    e. None of the above

22. RJR Nabisco sells its export receivables to a firm that takes responsibility for collecting payment from the importer. RJR has used
    a. accounts receivable financing.
    b. factoring.
    c. forfaiting.
    d. letter of credit.
    e. none of the above.

23. Who bears the payment risk in a letter of credit?
    a. The exporter
    b. The importer
    c. The issuing bank
    d. Both the exporter and the importer
    e. None of the above

24. Which of the following is a reason why commercial banks can facilitate international trade?
    a. The exporter may not wish to accept the credit risk of the importer.
    b. The government may impose exchange controls, thereby preventing payment by the importer to the exporter.
    c. The exporter may need financing until payment for the goods has been received.
    d. All of the above
    e. None of the above

Problems

25. L.A. Cellular has received an order for phone switches from Singapore. The switches will be exported under the terms of a letter of credit issued by Sumitomo Bank on behalf of Singapore Telecommunications. Under the terms of the L/C, the face value of the export order, $12 million, will be paid six months after Sumitomo accepts a draft drawn by L.A. Cellular. The current discount rate on 6-month acceptances is 8.5% p.a., and the acceptance fee is 1.25% p.a. How much will L.A. Cellular receive if it sells the acceptance at once?

    a. $11,850,000
    b. $11,415,000
    c. $10,980,000
    d. $10,830,000
    e. None of the above

26. Suppose Minnesota Machines (MM) is trying to price an export order from Russia. Payment is due nine months after shipping. Given the risks involved, MM would like to factor its receivable without recourse. The factor will charge a monthly discount of 2% plus a fee equal to 1.5% of the face value of the receivable for the nonrecourse financing. If MM desires revenues of $2.5 million from the sale, after paying all factoring charges, what is the minimum acceptable price it should charge?
    a. $2.59 million
    b. $2.67 million
    c. $2.70 million
    d. $2.79 million
    e. None of the above

Answers and Solutions

1. Foreign trade transactions

2. risks

3. greatest; cash

4. letter of credit

5. credit risk

6. irrevocable

7. confirmed

8. unconditional; sight draft; time draft

9. documents; drawee

10. currency controls

11. receipt; summary; title

12. commercial; consular invoices; insurance certificate

13. bill of exchange; time draft

14. banker's acceptance

15. Discounting

16. subsidized

17. Export-Import Bank

18. risk; competition

19. below

20. Countertrade

21. **c.** An exporter will prefer an irrevocable letter of credit by the importer's bank with confirmation by a domestic bank. Thus, the exporter can use a bank in its own country for compliance with the terms of the L/C.

22. **b.** When a firm sells its receivables to a factor for cash, it is using factoring.

23. **c.** Since the bank issuing the letter of credit guarantees payment, it assumes the credit risk.

24. **d.** Commercial banks facilitate international trade transactions whenever the exporter is unwilling to accept the credit risk of an importer, governments impose currency controls, and the exporter needs financing until payment is received.

25. **b.** Since L.A. Cellular can sell the acceptance at a 4.25% discount (8.5%/2), it will receive $11,415,000 immediately.

Face amount of acceptance	$12,000,000
Less: 1.25% p.a. acceptance fee for 6 months	75,000
Less: 8.5% p.a. discount for 6 months	510,000
Amount received immediately	$11,415,000

26. **c.** MM should charge a minimum acceptable price of $2.7 million to net $2.5 million from the factor.

$$x [1 - (1.5\% + 6\%)] = 2.5$$
$$x = 2.5/0.925$$
$$x = 2.7$$

CHAPTER 14

CURRENT ASSET MANAGEMENT

Overview

The principles and policies relating to working capital management for the multinational corporation are essentially the same as for the domestic firm. That is, both should maintain adequate levels of working capital to insure the smooth and trouble-free functioning of the firm, while avoiding unnecessary funds tied up in cash balances, marketable securities, accounts receivables, and inventories. The objective of effective working capital management for the multinational corporation as well as its domestic counterpart is the maximization of shareholder wealth. Multinational management of working capital, however, differs from domestic management by the wider choices of financing and investment options available, the additional risks of currency fluctuations and exchange controls, the different taxation systems and differential tax rates, and the ability to move funds among its various affiliates.

Outline

I. **The cash-positioning decision of a multinational corporation is identical to that of a purely domestic firm, but is complicated by the additional risks and opportunities.**

A. A multinational corporation can efficiently and quickly control its cash resources by establishing accurate and timely cash forecasts and reporting systems among its affiliates, improving the collection and disbursement of cash, and decreasing the cost of moving funds between its affiliates.

B. Optimizing the conservation and utilization of these funds is achieved by minimizing cash balances, making funds available when and where needed, and maximizing the risk-adjusted return on any excess funds.

C. The complexity of the international cash-positioning decision arises from government restrictions imposed on the free flow of funds, multiple taxation systems and currencies, and lack of internationally integrated interchange facilities.

D. Opportunities to improve global cash management include higher returns on short-term investments, lower applicable tax rates, and overall higher returns to the firm due to lower required levels of cash and marketable securities worldwide.

E. The key to developing an optimum cash management system is to centralize the cash-positioning function which affords the multinational corporation the following advantages:
1. Holding cash balances maintained throughout the system at a minimum.

2. Increasing profitability, while minimizing financing costs.
3. Improving the decision making process involved in making cash-positioning decisions.
4. Obtaining better foreign exchange quotes and financial services due to the large volume of foreign currency transactions.
5. Making efficient short-term investment decisions.
6. Reduced political risk.

F. Accelerating the collection of funds to reduce float is a key element of international cash management.
1. Cable remittances minimize delays in the receipt and conversion of payments into cash.
2. The SWIFT network improves the efficiency and reliability of international fund transfers among member banks.
3. Cash mobilization centers which are centrally located reduce mislocated funds.
4. A lock-box system reduces mail time and processing time.
5. Same-day value of funds by multinational banks or their correspondent networks speeds up the transfer of those funds.
6. The treasury workstation is a software package which links the firm to its bank and branch offices. Funds are transferred and recorded electronically within minutes.

G. Payments netting reduces the volume and cost of intercompany fund flows.
1. Netting involves offsetting receivables against payables of the various units, so that only the net amounts are transferred among affiliates.
2. Bilateral netting is used when two subsidiaries sell goods to each other.
3. Multilateral netting is valuable if companies have a relatively large volume of interaffiliate payments.
4. The netting center is a subsidiary usually set up in a location with minimal exchange controls for trade transactions. It coordinates the payment flows among the multinational corporation's various affiliates.
5. A netting system is useful to a multinational corporation only if restrictions on funds transfers are nonexistent. In some cases, permission from local monetary authorities must be obtained.
6. The higher the volume of intercompany transactions, the greater the value of netting to the multinational corporation.

H. The higher returns from short-term investments overseas must be traded off against the transactions costs involved.
1. The amount of funds available for investment depends on the cash needs of the company and its affiliates and the required minimum cash balances.
2. The choice of an appropriate short-term money market instrument is largely determined by government regulations, the structure of the market, and the foreign tax laws.
3. To reduce transactions costs, the currency denomination of near-term money is matched with foreign currency cash inflows and outflows.
4. Although the interest earned on these marketable securities is important, it is considered only after accounting for all the risks associated with an international short-term investment portfolio.

I. Centralization of international cash management involves some cash pooling which enables the firm to minimize its level of cash reserves to achieve a given financial safety level.

J. To successfully coordinate a firm's global cash and marketable securities, a good reporting system is needed.
1. With a cash mobilization system, the use of funds is optimized by tracking current and near-term cash positions.

2. Short-term periodical cash budgets, or cash forecasts, will enable the manager of the cash pool to make decisions with regard to the timing and amount of funds, the inflows and outflows in various currencies, the need for borrowing and required maturities, and the amount and duration of cash balances available for investment.

3. Cash reporting should be done in cleared funds, which is money available for immediate use.

4. The information from affiliate cash reports can be used to decide how to cover any deficits and where to invest surplus funds.

K. While good bank relations are important to effective cash management, many firms mismanage the relations with their banks. A bank audit can help the firm determine the value of any bank services they receive and the value of the business they generate for each bank they deal with.

II. **Firms make investments in receivables because they expect them to be profitable.**

A. By extending credit to customers, the firm expects to expand its sales volume or to retain customers which otherwise would be lost.
1. Credit terms set for customers in foreign countries should reflect the respective inflation rate.
2. Credit standards should be based on the practices used in the various countries, which often are more relaxed than in the United States.
3. In many companies, managers are rewarded for higher sales than penalized for an increased investment in receivables.

B. Accounts receivables overseas are better managed if salespeople understand how credit and collection affect the company's profits.

C. When granting trade credit to customers overseas, the firm must decide how much credit to extend and in which currency credit sales are to be billed.
1. Receivables overseas can be managed better if sales bonuses are adjusted to reflect the interest and currency costs of credit sales.
2. A multinational corporation may benefit from revised credit terms if different opinions exist regarding expected inflation and currency changes, credit can be obtained at lower risk-adjusted costs, or funds become suddenly available due to credit rationing in a country in which a subsidiary is located.

D. Firms should always compare the expected costs and benefits of extending credit internationally. This involves calculating incremental costs and incremental profits:

$$\Delta S - \Delta C \geq S \, \Delta R + \Delta S \, (R + \Delta R).$$

If, and only if, the incremental profits are greater than the incremental costs should the multinational corporation select a new credit policy.

III. **Managing inventories overseas is typically more difficult as well as realizing inventory turnover objectives.**

A. Firms have found that maintaining onshore manufacturing facilities is more efficient than setting up production overseas which results in higher inventory carrying costs.

B. Buying imported goods in advance allows companies to partially hedge their currency risk, particularly in countries where forward contracts are limited or nonexistent.

C. When faced with supply disruptions, companies will resort to inventory stockpiling through advance purchases. However, the cost associated with stockpiling inventory is quite high.

Fill-in-the-Blanks

1. The major differences between international and domestic working capital management include the impact of _____ _____, _____ _____ _____, and _____ ___ _____.

2. The _____ cash management objectives also apply to the international cash-positioning decision which include _____ cash resources as quickly and efficiently as possible and _____ the conservation and utilization of these funds.

3. There is a growing tendency for multinational corporations to _____ their cash management function.

4. Accelerating the collection of cash receipts minimizes the _____.

5. One approach for speeding up the collection process is setting up a ____ _____ center.

6. With _____, only the netted amount of any sales and purchases is transferred.

7. A multinational corporation needs to know whether governments _____ netting before it can implement a _____ _____ system.

8. The higher risk-adjusted returns on international short-term investments must be weighted against the _____ ____ involved.

9. A ____ ____ is a centrally managed account in which an affiliate's surplus cash is transferred.

10. The key to successful global coordination of a firm's ____ and _____ _____ is a good _____ system.

11. Good ____ _____ are important to the international cash management efforts of a firm.

12. When setting ____ ____, the multinational corporation must decide on the _____ of credit to be extended and the _____ in which the credit sales are to be billed.

13. A firm's credit policy should be adjusted only if _____ _____ are greater than _____ ____.

14. _____ _____ _____ can partially hedge a firm's currency risk if forward contracts are not available and can protect against supply disruptions.

15. Holding large amounts of _____ can be quite expensive.

Conceptual Questions

16. Netting can do all of the following except
    a. reduce foreign exchange risk.
    b. reduce foreign exchange costs.
    c. reduce float.
    d. reduce cable charges.
    e. none of the above.

17. An increase in the inflation rate is likely to
    a. raise interest rates.
    b. increase the demand for cash management services.
    c. lower the cost of collection float.
    d. all of the above
    e. a and b only

18. By centralizing affiliate credit policy and monitoring collection performance, parent companies can
    a. reduce the investment in accounts receivables.
    b. reduce foreign exchange and other transaction costs.
    c. reduce banking fees.
    d. reduce float.
    e. all of the above

Problems

19. Suppose the current value of the Greek drachma is $0.006369, but the expected spot rate in 90 days is $0.005980. What is the value of a sales order of Dr 50 million sold on 90-day terms?
    a. $318,450
    b. $562,491
    c. $299,000
    d. $415,430
    e. None of the above

20. Newport Circuits is trying to decide whether to shift production overseas of its relatively expensive integrated circuits (they average around $11 each). Offshore assembly would save about 8.2 cents per chip in labor costs. But by producing offshore, it would take about five weeks to get the parts to customers in contrast to one week with domestic manufacturing. Thus, offshore production would force Newport to carry another four weeks of inventory. In addition, offshore production would entail combined shipping and customs duty costs of 3.2 cents. Suppose Newport's cost of funds is 15%. How much money will Newport save per chip by shifting production offshore?
    a. $0.05
    b. $0.032
    c. $0.013
    d. $0.027
    e. Nothing. It will cost Newport an additional $0.077 per chip to shift production offshore.

Answers and Solutions

1. currency fluctuations; potential exchange controls; multiple tax jurisdictions

2. domestic; controlling; optimizing

3. centralize

4. float

5. cash mobilization

6. netting

7. restrict; multilateral payments

8. transaction costs

9. cash pool

10. cash; marketable securities; reporting

11. bank relations

12. credit terms; amount; currency

13. incremental profits; incremental costs

14. Advance inventory purchases

15. inventory

16. **a.** While netting can reduce foreign exchange costs, transaction costs, cable charges, and float, it does not eliminate exchange rate risk.

17. **e.** As the inflation rate increases, interest rates go up and the demand for cash management services increases.

18. **e.** To better manage accounts receivables, a firm should centralize its affiliate's credit policies and monitor its collection performance. As a result, the investment in receivables is reduced as well as foreign exchange and other transactions costs, banking fees, and float.

19. **c.** The value of a sales order of Dr 50 million sold on 90-day terms is $299,000 or

$$Dr\ 50,000,000 \times \$0.005980 = \$299,000.$$

20. **e.** By shifting production offshore, Newport would incur an additional cost of $0.077. This is calculated as follows:

    (1) The net benefit of shifting production overseas is equal to the labor cost savings - (shipping + customs duty + cost of money tied up in inventory).

(2) The key here is to compute the final term. By producing abroad, Newport is forced to carry another four weeks of inventory. At an annual cost of funds equal to 15% and an average cost per chip of $11, the added inventory-related interest expense due to offshore production is found as follows:

Added interest expense = opportunity cost of funds $\times$ added time in transit $\times$ cost/part

$$= 0.15 \times (4/52) \times \$11.00$$
$$= \$0.1269.$$

Thus, the net benefit to Newport of offshore production equals

$$8.2¢ - (3.2¢ + 12.7¢) = -7.7¢.$$

Hence, it is not worthwhile to shift production abroad. The high inventory cost alone will more than offset the labor cost savings.

CHAPTER 15

MANAGING THE MULTINATIONAL FINANCIAL SYSTEM

Overview

A unique characteristic of the multinational corporation is its ability to transfer funds and reallocate profits between its various foreign affiliates. By using internal financial transfer mechanisms, the firm can minimize taxes and avoid exchange rate risk, circumvent exchange controls and blockage of funds, and access financial markets for capital which otherwise would not be available. Financial decisions associated with the use of such techniques are highly complex because of the conflicting nature of corporate objectives. For example, if blocked funds are removed from a low-tax country, the firm's worldwide tax liability is likely to increase. Similarly, if exchange rate risk is reduced, interest expenses may be higher which adds to the financing needs of subsidiaries in soft-currency nations. The emphasis to be placed on each of these goals is determined by the individual impact of each goal on corporate profitability.

Outline

I. **The multinational financial system enables multinational corporations to arbitrage tax systems, financial markets, and regulatory systems.**

   A. Tax arbitrage arises when wide variations in national tax systems allow firms to reduce their tax bill by moving funds from affiliates located in high tax countries to those located in low tax countries. Profits can also be reallocated internally from subsidiaries with taxpaying positions to those with tax losses.

   B. Financial market arbitrage arises when imperfections in these markets enable firms to avoid exchange controls, earn higher risk-adjusted returns on surplus funds, reduce risk-adjusted borrowing costs, and access previously unavailable capital markets by using internal funds mechanisms.

   C. Regulatory system arbitrage arises when regulations in different countries rather than the marketplace determine subsidiary profits. In this case, the firm can disguise the true profitability of its affiliates by transferring accounting profits among its units, thereby gaining a negotiating advantage with foreign governments or unions.

II. **The transfer of funds from affiliates to the parent and from one affiliate to another takes many different forms.**

   A. Unbundling, a policy followed by many multinational corporations, is breaking up total intracorporate transfer of funds into separate flows which corresponds to the nature of the payment.

1. Dividends, interest, and repayment of principal can be matched against the capital invested in the form of debt or equity.
2. Fees, royalties, and corporate overhead can be charged for various corporate services, trademarks, or licenses.
3. Internal financial transfer mechanisms available to the multinational corporation include transfer pricing, fee and royalty adjustments, leading and lagging, intracorporate loans, dividend adjustments, and overseas funds investments as debt or equity.

B. Total tax payments on internal fund transfers depend on the tax regulations of both the host and the recipient countries.
   1. The host country typically imposes two types of taxes, a corporate income tax and a withholding tax on dividend, interest, and fee remittances.
   2. Some countries, such as Germany and Japan, charge a tax on retained earnings instead of dividends.
   3. The United States and many other recipient nations tax income remitted from foreign countries at the regular corporate income tax rate. If the domestic corporate income tax rate is higher than the foreign tax rate, parent companies must pay an incremental tax cost on remitted dividends and other payments.
   4. To offset the additional taxes paid on foreign earned income, most countries, including the United States, provide foreign tax credits.
   5. For example, if a foreign subsidiary has generated $100,000 in earnings before taxes and the foreign corporate tax rate is 55%, while in the United States it is 34%, the subsidiary will have to pay taxes of $55,000 to the host government. Suppose the difference of $45,000 is remitted to the parent as dividends. At this point, U.S. corporate taxes are imposed on the foreign earnings of $100,000. But since the foreign tax rate is higher than the U.S. corporate tax rate, the parent will receive a foreign tax credit of $21,000 [$100,000 (0.55 - 0.34) = $21,000].

C. Multinational corporations can use the transfer pricing mechanism to reduce taxes and tariffs, avoid exchange controls, increase their shares of profit from a joint venture, and disguise profitability.
   1. If the corporate objective is to minimize taxes, then transfer prices for goods and services will have to be set so that, in effect, profits are being moved from a higher to a lower tax country. The following rule of thumb can be used when setting the transfer price for goods sold by subsidiary A to subsidiary B subject to their respective marginal tax rates:

   Set the transfer price as low as possible if $t_A > t_B$.
   Set the transfer price as high as possible if $t_A < t_B$.

   2. The transfer pricing decision is complicated with the introduction of tariffs. For example, suppose that an ad-valorem import duty is levied on the invoice price of goods shipped to subsidiary B from subsidiary A. Since this tariff is set as a percentage of the value of the imported goods, raising the transfer price will increase the import duty to be paid by subsidiary B. Thus, in general, if the ad-valorem tariff is higher relative to the income tax differential, then it is more desirable to set a low transfer price.
   3. Multinational corporations' use of transfer pricing to reduce the overall corporate tax bill is constrained by tax provisions in the United States and in most industrial countries. For example, Section 482 of the United States IRS code issues guidelines for ascertaining a correct price for intracorporate transactions. This price is based on the price used in the sale of the same goods to outside customers in an arm's length transaction. United States tax authorities have established four methods for setting an arm's length price.

a. The comparable uncontrolled price method establishes the most straightforward and most objective price; it is the price used in a similar transaction between two unrelated firms.

b. The resale price method determines the arm's length price as the sales price charged by an independent distributor less an appropriate profit margin.

c. The cost-plus method is based on the cost incurred by the manufacturer plus an appropriate markup.

d. Another appropriate method for determining the arm's length price is to use a combination of the above methods or use still another method (e.g., comparable profits and net yield method).

4. While transfer pricing can be used to achieve a number of important corporate objectives, it distorts the actual profits generated by a foreign subsidiary and, thus, creates difficulties in evaluating the performance of managers.

D. Large multinational corporations use reinvoicing centers located at tax havens to disguise profitability, avoid government regulations, and coordinate transfer pricing policy.

1. Reinvoicing centers take title to all goods sold by the parent to its affiliates, or by one affiliate to other affiliates, and invoice the receiving affiliates at prices set administratively to accomplish one or more corporate objectives.

2. The physical flow of goods from purchasing units to receiving units is not changed in any way.

3. The basic purpose of this arrangement is to funnel profits arising from these transactions to lower tax affiliates and away from the higher-taxed parent or affiliate. It is also used to position funds in countries with strong or stable currencies and/or no exchange controls and away from those with soft currencies and/or foreign exchange restrictions.

4. Reinvoicing centers, which were popular with U.S. multinational corporations prior to 1962, were discouraged by the passage of the U.S. Revenue Act of 1962, which declared that income realized by these centers is Subpart F income and, hence, is subject to U.S. taxation.

5. A 1977 ruling by the IRS, however, revived the use of reinvoicing centers by allocating to a firm's foreign subsidiaries certain parent expenses that previously could be written off only in the United States. Thus, additional foreign tax credits can be generated and be utilized only against U.S. taxes owed on foreign-source income.

E. Fees and royalties are often a more convenient way of accessing a foreign affiliate's profits.

1. Royalties represent payment for technological know-how, patents, and trademarks. Fees are compensation for professional services.

2. Firms determine fee and royalty charges most commonly by deciding on a desired amount of total fees to be remitted.

3. Host countries are less likely to impede or restrict funds transferred in payment for royalties and fees under a clear and specific written agreement than under an ambiguous one.

4. Multinational corporations tend to follow a stable remittance policy for fees and royalties.

F. Leading and lagging of interaffiliate payments is a common method of moving funds from one unit to another.

1. The value of leading and lagging is determined by the opportunity cost of funds to both the paying and receiving units.

2. With leading and lagging no formal debt obligation is needed, governments are less likely to interfere, and no interest rates are charged up to six months.

3. However, government regulations on intercompany credit terms are often tight and can change quickly.

G. Intercompany loans are valuable to multinational corporations if credit rationing, exchange controls, or differences in national tax rates exist.

1. A direct loan involves extending credit from the parent to an affiliate or from one affiliate to another without an intermediary.

2. A back-to-back loan, also called fronting loan or link financing, is an intercompany loan channeled through a bank. In this arrangement, the parent deposits funds with a bank in country A which, in turn, makes the money available to an affiliate located in country B. This loan is riskfree from the viewpoint of the bank, because it is collateralized by the parent's deposit. The bank simply fronts the loan for the parent, thereby providing protection against expropriation and/or currency controls. Back-to-back loans can also be used to reduce taxes and to access blocked funds without physically transferring them.

3. A parallel loan consists of two related but separate borrowings which usually involves four parties in two different countries. It is used to repatriate blocked funds, circumvent exchange controls, avoid premium exchange rates for foreign investments, finance foreign operations without incurring additional currency risk, or obtain foreign currency financing at attractive rates.

H. Dividends are the most important means of transferring funds from foreign affiliates to the parent.

1. The dividend decision for foreign affiliates is heavily influenced by the effective tax rates on dividend payments, financial statement effects, financing requirements, availability and cost of funds, exchange controls, currency risk, and the parent company's dividend payout ratio.

2. By varying dividend payout ratios among foreign subsidiaries, the multinational corporation can reduce its overall corporate tax liability.

3. An established track record of paying dividends consistently can reduce the threat of government interference with these payments.

I. Multinational corporations can realize several advantages from investing funds overseas in the form of loans rather than equity.

1. It is easier for a firm to repatriate funds in the form of interest and principal payments rather than as dividends or equity reductions, because the latter fund transfers are more closely controlled by foreign governments.

2. Intercompany loans can also reduce taxes because the interest paid on loans is tax-deductible in the host country, while dividends are not tax-deductible, and, unlike dividends, loan repayments to the parent do not represent taxable income.

3. Parent company loans to foreign affiliates are often regarded as equity investments by the host nations and their local creditors.

4. A multinational corporation is not completely free in choosing appropriate debt-equity ratios for its subsidiaries. The capital structure decision is often subject to government negotiations. In addition, dividends and local financing are frequently restricted to a fixed percentage of the firm's equity base.

5. To determine the amount of equity for a subsidiary, firms normally use guidelines, such as 50% of total assets or fixed assets.

J. The currency selection in which intracorporate transactions are invoiced has both tax effects and exchange control implications.

1. The invoicing currency or currencies can affect after-tax profits if currency movements are anticipated. Thus, in general, interaffiliate transactions should be denominated so that exchange rate gains are realized in low-tax countries and exchange rate losses in high-tax countries. Note, though, that the net gain from these transactions is zero if taxes are ignored.

2. The option of selecting the invoicing currency can also enable a firm to remove some blocked funds from a country which imposes currency and capital controls.

III. **Use of the various financial linkages must be coordinated in a manner consistent with the financial goal of maximizing shareholder wealth.**

A. Multinational corporations can take advantage of their internal financial systems by conducting a systematic and comprehensive analysis of the options available for remitting funds and their associated costs and benefits.

B. Most firms tend to satisfice rather than optimize the use of their internal financial links.

C. The value of the internal financial transfer system to the multinational corporation depends on the volume of intercompany transactions, the number of financial linkages, the pattern of foreign affiliate ownership, the degree of product and service standardization, and the existence of government regulations.

D. To operate an integrated global system successfully, the firm needs detailed information on the financing requirements of its subsidiaries, the sources and costs of external capital, the yields on local investments, the available financial channels, the volume of intersubsidiary transactions, all relevant tax factors, and government restrictions and regulations imposed on fund transfers.

E. As firms manipulate transfer prices on goods and services, adjust dividend payments, and delay or speed up remittances, profits and liquidity are shifted among the firm's various units. While after-tax global profits are increased by corporate intervention, incentive systems based on profit centers may be destroyed.

IV. **The blockage of funds by actions of host governments, as discussed in the appendix, is a common phenomenon in many LDCs which normally face chronic or temporary balance of payments disequilibria. Strategies used by multinational corporations to deal with transfer blockage may be handled in the following three stages: (a) defensive strategies against anticipated blockage of funds or restrictions before undertaking the foreign project; (b) measures to manage recurrent partial blockage of funds from an ongoing operation; and (c) strategies to handle total and prolonged blockage of funds or forced reinvestment so that the value of those blocked funds is maintained.**

Fill-in-the-Blanks

1. _____ _____ _____ _____ enable multinational corporations to shift funds and accounting profits among its foreign affiliates.

2. The value of a firm's network of financial linkages stems from three arbitrage opportunities: ___ _____, _____ ____ _____, and _____ ____ _____.

3. _____ involves separating the total flow of funds into components that are associated with the resources transferred in the form of products and services, capital, and technology.

4. By shifting funds from ____-___ nations to ___-___ nations, the multinational corporation can reduce its overall corporate tax liability.

5. _____ _____ can be used to avoid currency controls.

6. The most appropriate method for determining the arm's length price is the _____ _____ ____ method.

7. A _____ _____ takes title of all goods sold by the parent to another affiliate or between affiliates without changing the physical flow of the goods from the factory to the purchaser.

8. Fees and royalties are charged for _____ _____ __ _____, such as professional advice from the parent, allocated overhead, patents, and trademarks.

9. Leading and lagging of interaffiliate payments is accomplished by modifying the _____ _____ extended by one subsidiary to another.

10. _____ _____ are loans directly provided by the parent to a foreign affiliate without the use of an _____.

11. In a _____-__-_____ loan, the parent deposits funds in a foreign bank which is used as _____ for a loan extended to an affiliate located in another foreign country.

12. An increase in the payment of _____ can lead to a decrease in total U.S. taxes.

13. The best way to increase the present value of after-tax remittances from abroad is to invest funds in the form of ____ rather than _____.

14. Choosing ____-__-____ ratios is open for negotiations with the ____ governments.

15. The option of invoicing currencies has both ___ and _____ _____ implications.

16. Coordinating the use of various _____ _____ requires decisions about the amount and timing of remittances, receiving units, and available channels.

17. Multinational corporations tend to _____ rather than _____ the use of transfer mechanisms.

18. The value of a firm's global financial system depends on the _____ of financial links and the _____ of intercompany transactions.

19. _____ _____ simultaneously motivate and constrain the use of funds transfer techniques by multinationals.

Conceptual Questions

20. A common purpose of interaffiliate leading and lagging is to
    a. allow affiliates with excess funds to provide financing to affiliates with deficient funds.
    b. assure that the inventory levels at affiliates are maintained within tolerable ranges.
    c. change the prices that a high-tax rate affiliate charges a low-tax affiliate.
    d. measure the performance of affiliates according to how quickly affiliates remit dividend payments to the parent.
    e. none of the above

21. A basic reason for the transfer pricing problems faced by many multinational corporations is that
    a. managers in the various subsidiaries do not understand how their behavior affects the rest of the company.
    b. multinationals sometimes fail to decouple the transfer prices used for tax purposes from the transfer prices used for performance evaluation purposes.
    c. tax and tariff authorities are becoming more alert.
    d. all of the above
    e. none of the above

22. Subsidiaries A and B buy from and sell to each other. Suppose that A has excess cash, whereas B is short of cash. How can A funnel funds to B?
    a. A can lead payments owed to B.
    b. B can lag payments owed to A.
    c. A can raise transfer prices on goods sold to B.
    d. All of the above
    e. a and b only

Problems

23. Suppose a firm earns $2.5 million before tax in Spain. It pays Spanish taxes of $1.3 million and remits the remaining $1.2 million as a dividend to its U.S. parent. The Spanish dividend withholding tax is 5%. Under current U.S. tax law, the parent will owe on this dividend U.S. taxes of
    a. $1.15 million.
    b. $552,000.
    c. nothing. It will also receive a foreign tax credit equal to $1.3 million.
    d. nothing. It will also receive a foreign tax credit equal to $510,000.
    e. none of the above.

24. Suppose affiliate A sells goods worth $1 million monthly to affiliate B on 30-day credit terms. A switch in credit terms to 120 days will involve a one-time shift in cash of
    a. $3 million from A to B.
    b. $3 million from B to A.
    c. $4 million from A to B.
    d. $4 million from B to A.
    e. none of the above.

25. Suppose affiliate A sells 10,000 chips monthly to affiliate B at a unit price of $15. Affiliate A's tax rate is 45%, and affiliate B's tax rate is 55%. In addition, affiliate B must pay an ad-valorem tariff of 12% on its imports. If the transfer price on chips can be set anywhere between $11 and $18, how much can the total monthly cash flow of A and B be increased by switching to the optimal transfer price?
    a. $4,960
    b. $3,600
    c. $1,380
    d. $1,620
    e. None of the above

Answers and Solutions

1. Internal financial transfer mechanisms

2. tax arbitrage; financial market arbitrage; regulatory system arbitrage

3. Unbundling

4. high-tax; low-tax

5. Transfer pricing

6. comparable uncontrolled price

7. reinvoicing center

8. intangible factors of production

9. credit terms

10. Direct loans; intermediary

11. back-to-back; collateral

12. dividends

13. debt; equity

14. debt-to-equity; host

15. tax; currency control

16. financial linkages

17. satisfy; optimize

18. number; volume

19. Government regulations

20. **a.** Leading and lagging can be used to shift surplus funds from an affiliate to one which is short of funds.

21. **b.** While transfer pricing distorts profits of reporting units, it also creates difficulties in evaluating managerial performance. This problem arises because managers are typically evaluated on the basis of profits. But if transfer prices are adjusted to reduce overall corporate taxes, managers may behave in ways that lead to suboptimal decision-making which affects the corporation as a whole.

22. **e.** As affiliate A speeds up the payment of intercompany transactions with B, money is quickly shifted to the deficit unit. On the other hand, as affiliate B delays the payments owed to A, it has access to funds which otherwise would not be available.

23. **d.** According to U.S. tax law, the firm's U.S. taxes owed on the dividend payment is calculated as follows:

Dividend	$1,200,000
Spanish tax paid	1,300,000

Included in U.S. taxable income	$2,500,000
U.S. tax @ 34%	850,000
Less U.S. indirect tax credit	1,300,000
Less Spanish dividend withholding tax @ 5%	60,000

Net U.S. tax owed	($ 510,000)

Because the Spanish tax rate is greater than the U.S. tax rate and a withholding tax on dividends has been imposed by the Spanish government, the company receives a foreign tax credit of $510,000 that can be used to offset U.S. taxes owed on other foreign source income.

24. **a.** If affiliate A changes credit terms so that affiliate B can delay payments by an additional 90 days, it will receive a one-time shift of funds from A in the amount of $3,000,000 or

$$(120 - 30)/30 \times \$1,000,000 = \$3,000,000.$$

25. **c.** For each $1 increase in income shifted from B to A, A's taxes rise by $0.45. At the same time, B must pay an extra $0.12 in tariffs. The before-tax increase of $1.12 in B's cost gives it a tax write-off worth $0.616 or $1.12 \times 0.55 = \$0.616$. By shifting $1 in income from B to A, the effect is to lower B's tax payments by $0.616 and raise its tariffs by $0.12, a net decrease in tax plus tariff payments of $0.496. The net effect of switching $1 in income from B to A is to lower tax plus tariff payments to the world by $0.496 - $0.45 = $0.046. Thus, the transfer price should be set as high as possible in order to shift as much income as possible to A from B. The new transfer price should, therefore, be set at $18, a $3 increase over the old transfer price. The resulting increase in monthly cash flows is $1,380 or [$0.046 \times \$3 \times 10,000 = \$1,380].

CHAPTER 16

INTERNATIONAL PORTFOLIO INVESTMENT

Overview

As capital markets become more integrated, investors can diversify their portfolios internationally rather than just domestically. International stock and bond investments offer substantially higher returns with reduced risk compared to investments in a single market only. A major reason is that international investments broaden the opportunity locus from which investors select their optimal international portfolios. Another important reason is that security returns across countries are less positively correlated than those from within a country. Thus, a diversified international portfolio will be less risky than a U.S. portfolio that is fully diversified. An investor restricted to domestic investments would, in effect, be cut off from over two-thirds of the available investment opportunities.

Outline

I. **The total dollar return from foreign investments consists of dividend or interest income, capital gains or losses, and currency gains or losses.**

A. A foreign bond investment for a one-year holding period provides a total dollar return of

$$1 + R_\$ = \left[1 + \frac{B(1) - B(0) + C}{B(0)}\right](1 + g)$$

That is, the total dollar return is equal to the foreign currency return times the currency gain or loss.
1. For example, suppose the price of British bonds moved from £102 to £106, while paying a coupon of £9. At the same time, the pound sterling moved from \$1.62 to \$1.76. The total dollar return from this bond investment is 22.49% calculated as follows:

$$R_\$ = [1 + (£106 - £102 + £9)/£102] (1 + 0.0864) - 1 = 0.2249.$$

2. From the equation, it can be seen that the currency gain applies to both the foreign currency principal and the foreign currency return.

B. A foreign stock investment with a one-year holding period provides a total dollar return of

$$1 + R_\$ = \left[1 + \frac{P(1) - P(0) + DIV}{P(0)}\right](1 + g)$$

1. For example, suppose that, during the year, Toyota Motor Company shares moved from ¥9,000 to ¥11,000, while paying a dividend of ¥60. At the same time, the exchange rate moved from ¥120 to ¥145. The total dollar return from this investment is 1.7%, which is computed as follows:

$$R_\$ = [1 + (¥11,000 - ¥9,000 + ¥60)/¥9,000] (1 - 0.1724) - 1 = 0.017.$$

2. In this example, the investor suffered both a capital loss on the foreign currency principal and a currency loss on the dollar value of the investment.

C. Foreign currency fluctuations introduce exchange rate risk in foreign security investments.
  1. The dollar rate of return on a foreign investment is approximately equal to the foreign currency rate of return plus the change in the dollar value of the foreign currency or

$$R_\$ = R_f + g.$$

  2. The standard deviation of the dollar return is calculated as shown:

$$\sigma_\$ = [\sigma_f^2 + \sigma_g^2 + 2\sigma_f\sigma_g\sigma_{f,g}]^{1/2}$$

  3. A sufficiently large negative correlation between the rate of exchange rate change and the foreign currency return could lower the risk of international investing.

II. **International investments offer numerous advantages to investors.**

A. With increased investment opportunities, investors can achieve a better risk-return trade-off than by investing only in domestic portfolios.
  1. The broader the diversification, the more stable the portfolio returns and the greater the reduction in portfolio risk.
  2. By diversifying portfolios across countries whose economic cycles are not perfectly correlated, investors are able to reduce still further the variability of their returns.
  3. Investing in emerging markets can reduce portfolio risk despite high investment risk because of their low correlations with returns elsewhere.

B. The benefits of international equity investments appear to be substantial. Solnik (1974) and Lessard (1976) both have found empirically that national factors have a significant influence on security returns relative to that of any common world factor. They also found a low correlation between equity returns from different national financial markets, which can be largely explained by local monetary and fiscal policies, differences in institutional and legal systems, and regional economic shocks.

C. A foreign market beta is a measure of market risk which is derived from the capital asset pricing model. It is calculated relative to the U.S. market in the same way as is an individual asset beta:

$$\text{Foreign market beta} = \text{Correlation with U.S. market} \times \frac{\text{Standard deviation of foreign market}}{\text{Standard deviation of U.S. market}}$$

For example, if the correlation between the West German market is 0.31, and the standard deviation of the German market and U.S. market is 19.4% and 18.2%, respectively, then the German market beta is 0.31 x (19.4/18.2) = 0.33.

D. Much of the risk associated with individual markets is unsystematic and, thus, can be diversified away.

E. In recent years, foreign investments have been more profitable than investing in only the U.S. market. A major reason for this trend is that international diversification broadens the investment opportunities, thus pushing out the efficient frontier. As a result, investors are able to simultaneously increase their expected returns and reduce their risk.

F. The benefits of international diversification can be estimated by considering the portfolio risk and portfolio return in which a fraction, a, is invested in U.S. stocks and the remaining fraction, $1 - a$, is invested in foreign stocks.
1. The expected portfolio return is calculated as follows:

$$r_p = a\, r_{us} + (1 - a)\, r_{rw}.$$

2. The portfolio standard deviation is calculated as shown:

$$\sigma_P = [a^2\sigma_{us}^2 + (1-a)^2\sigma_{rw}^2 + 2a(1-a)\sigma_{us}\sigma_{rw}\sigma_{us,rw}]^{1/2}$$

3. The risk of an internationally diversified portfolio is less than the risk of a fully diversified U.S. portfolio.

G. International diversification is of benefit only if the correlation among assets is relatively low. Recent research has found that the correlation between U.S. and non-U.S. equity markets is somewhat higher today than during previous periods, thereby reducing the advantages of international investing.

H. Another caveat of global investing is that when markets are the most volatile, and investors most seek safety, international diversification is of limited value.

I. Investing in emerging markets offers high returns and has high risks. Although these markets are located in countries characterized by volatile economic and political prospects, they offer the greatest diversification benefits at reduced portfolio risk because of their low correlations with returns elsewhere.

J. The value of international diversification is reduced by barriers to investing overseas. Such barriers do exist and include segmented capital markets, lack of liquidity, exchange controls, less developed foreign capital markets, exchange rate risk, and lack of readily accessible and comparable information.

K. U.S. investors can diversify into foreign securities by buying foreign stocks listed on the NYSE or buying foreign stocks overseas. An alternative to purchasing securities in foreign markets is to buy foreign equities in the form of American Depository Receipts (ADRs) or American shares.
1. ADRs are negotiable certificates issued by a U.S. bank to represent the underlying shares it holds in custody.
2. American shares are certificates issued by a transfer agent in the United States acting on behalf of the foreign issuer.

L. Internationally diversified mutual funds provide a convenient as well as low-cost financial instrument for international investing. The following four types of mutual funds invest abroad:
1. Global funds invest anywhere in the world, including the United States.
2. International funds invest only in foreign countries.
3. Regional funds invest in specific geographic areas overseas.
4. Single-currency funds invest in individual countries.

III. Internationally diversified bond portfolios offer superior investment performance.

A. Barnett and Rosenberg (1983) examined the portfolio returns from domestic and international bond investments. They found that the inclusion of foreign bonds in a portfolio provided higher returns than a U.S. bond portfolio. In addition, the volatility of the portfolio fell reflecting the low correlation between U.S. and foreign bond returns.

B. Other studies examining different time periods support Barnett and Rosenberg's findings, suggesting that internationally diversified bond portfolios outperform U.S. bond portfolios.

IV. International stock and bond diversification together provide a better risk-return trade-off than either alone.

A. Solnik and Noetzling (1982) studied the benefits of international stock and bond diversification. By comparing the performances of various investment strategies over the period 1970-1980, they found that:
1. portfolio returns from foreign stock investments offered better risk-return trade-offs.
2. portfolios with international stock and bond investments had substantially less risk than international equity portfolios alone.
3. risk-return trade-offs can be greatly improved by internationally diversifying stock and bond investments with proportions that are not consistent with relative market capitalizations.

B. Optimal investment in international securities enables investors to double or even triple the returns realized from investing in index funds without incurring more risk.

Fill-in-the-Blanks

1. The total dollar return on international bond and stock investments equals the _____ _____ _____ times the _____ ____ or ____.

2. International diversification provides a better _____ _____ than investing in _____ securities only.

3. Investments in foreign stocks can greatly _____ risk because of the ___ correlation between foreign and domestic equity returns.

4. A large portion of the risk associated with individual markets is _____.

5. Because of increased investment opportunities, the _____ _____ is pushed out.

6. _____ to investing abroad limit the benefits of international diversification.

7. U.S. investors can buy _____ _____ _____ or _____ _____ instead of purchasing foreign securities in overseas markets directly.

8. Internationally diversified _____ _____ provide low-cost vehicles for international investing.

9. _____ _____ which have been diversified internationally deliver superior performance.

10. _____ foreign stocks and bonds in a portfolio yields a _____ risk-return trade-off than either one alone.

Conceptual Questions

11. International diversification provides a better risk-return trade-off than does investing solely in U.S. securities primarily because
    a. many foreign industries do not exist in the United States.
    b. there are many more securities to choose from overseas.
    c. the economic cycles of nations are not perfectly in phase.
    d. all of the above.
    e. a and b only.

12. The greatest diversification gains can be achieved by
    a. adding more domestic stocks to a portfolio.
    b. substituting foreign stocks for domestic stocks.
    c. substituting foreign stocks and bonds for domestic stocks.
    d. substituting foreign bonds for domestic stocks.
    e. none of the above.

13. The benefits of international diversification are limited by the lack of _____ in foreign markets.
    a. liquidity
    b. free convertibility of many currencies
    c. adequate information
    d. all of the above
    e. b and c only

Problems

14. A Thai baht bond with a coupon of 9.5% is initially priced at its face value of Bt1,000. At the end of one year, the bond is selling for Bt1,050. If the initial spot rate was Bt25/$, at what end-of-year exchange rate will the dollar return on the bond just equal 10%?
    a. Bt 1 = $0.0384
    b. Bt 1 = $0.0416
    c. Bt 1 = $0.0482
    d. Bt 1 = $0.0324
    e. None of the above

15. The Japanese market has a correlation of 0.38 with the U.S. market and a standard deviation of return of 20.5%. What is the Japanese market's beta relative to the U.S. market? The standard deviation of return for the U.S. market is 18.2%.

  a. 0.72
  b. 1.39
  c. 0.86
  d. 0.43
  e. None of the above

16. Suppose you buy a share of Siemens at a price of DM 83. During the year, you receive a dividend of DM 2, and the DM appreciates by 8%. If the stock price at the end of the year is DM 80, what was your total dollar return for the year?
  a. 10.60%
  b. 6.70%
  c. 9.83%
  d. 8.43%
  e. None of the above

17. Suppose that the dollar is now worth DM 1.6372. If one-year German bunds are yielding 9.8% and one-year U.S. Treasury bonds are yielding 6.5%, at what end-of-year exchange rate will the dollar returns on the two bonds be equal?
  a. 1.5865
  b. 1.5880
  c. 1.6878
  d. 1.6896
  e. None of the above

18. Suppose that the standard deviation of the return on Nestlé, a Swiss firm, in terms of Swiss francs is 19%, and the standard deviation of the rate of change in the dollar-franc exchange rate is 15%. In addition, the estimated correlation between the Swiss franc return on Nestlé and the rate of change in the exchange rate is 0.17. What is the standard deviation of the dollar rate of return on investing in Nestlé stock?
  a. 6.83%
  b. 26.13%
  c. 34.00%
  d. 59.13%
  e. None of the above

Answers and Solutions

1. local currency return; currency gain; loss

2. risk-return trade-off; domestic

3. reduce; low

4. diversifiable

5. efficient frontier

6. Barriers

7. American Depository Receipts; American shares

8. mutual funds

9. Bond portfolios

10. Combining; better

11. **c.** By diversifying across countries whose economic cycles are not perfectly in phase, investors are able to reduce still further the variability of their returns with less risk.

12. **c.** International stock and bond diversification together offer a better risk-return trade-off than either alone.

13. **d.** The value of international investing is limited by the existence of barriers, such as lack of liquidity, exchange controls, and inadequate and incomparable information.

14. **a.** The end-of-year exchange rate must be $0.0384/Bt for the total dollar return on the bond to be 10%. This is computed as follows:

$$1.10 = [1 + (1,050 - 1,000 + 95)/1,000] (1 + x)$$
$$1.10 = 1.145 (1 + x)$$
$$x = -0.0393.$$

The end-of-year exchange rate is $(1/25) (1 - 0.0393) = \$0.0384$.

15. **d.** The Japanese market beta is $(0.38) (20.5/18.2) = 0.43$.

16. **b.** The total dollar return on a share of Siemens was 6.70% which is computed as follows:

$$R_\$ = [1 + (80 - 83 + 2)/83] (1 + 0.08) - 1$$
$$= (0.98795) (1.08) - 1$$
$$= 0.06698.$$

17. **c.** The end-of-year exchange rate of the dollar against the DM must be 1.6878 for the dollar return on the two bonds to be equal. This is computed as follows:

$$(1.065) = (1.098) (1 + g)$$
$$g = (1.065/1.098) - 1$$
$$g = -0.03$$

The end-of-year exchange rate is $[1.6372/(1 - 0.03)] = $ DM 1.6878/$.

18. **b.** The standard deviation of the dollar rate of return on investing in Nestlé is 26.13%, which is calculated as follows:

$$Ó_\$ \text{ (Nestlé)} = [(0.19^2 + 0.15^2 + (2)(0.19)(0.15)(0.17)]1/2 = 0.2613.$$

CHAPTER 17

CORPORATE STRATEGY AND FOREIGN DIRECT INVESTMENT

Overview

Becoming multinational is the last step in the overseas expansion process which begins with exporting. But, as foreign projects continue to provide excess returns and competitive pressures increase, multinational corporations must develop global strategies which will enable them to maintain their competitive advantage both at home and abroad. The focus of any successful strategy is to search for and then capitalize on imperfections in product and factor markets. These imperfections which prevent the free flow of goods and capital internationally have been created by governments through regulations and controls or by corporations through product differentiation supported by aggressive promotion. Only if a multinational corporation understands the factors that lead to success can it determine which foreign investments are likely to increase the value of shareholder wealth.

Outline

I. **The existence of multinational corporations can be traced to market imperfections.**

   A. According to the theory of industrial organization, a multinational firm operating as an oligopolist undertakes foreign direct investment to take advantage of product and factor market imperfections. In many cases, these imperfections have been created by the firm itself through its intangible capital which takes the form of technological know-how, general marketing skills, and organizational skills.

   B. Foreign direct investment or internalization is most likely where contractual difficulties make it costly to deal with unrelated foreign companies.
      1. With vertical integration, a multinational corporation can substitute internal production and distribution systems for inefficient markets.
      2. With horizontal integration, the firm can take advantage of its intangible capital and thus avoid contractual difficulties with unrelated parties.

   C. Financial market imperfections reduce a firm's riskiness through its ability to diversify internationally.

II. **Multinational corporations develop strategies to defend and exploit those entry barriers which have been created by imperfections in product and factor markets.**

   A. Firms create barriers to entry through product innovation and product differentiation.

B. As industries mature, economies of scale and economies of scope replace technological leads as barriers to entry.

C. Many multinational corporations take advantage of the learning curve to lower costs and drive out actual and potential competitors.

D. A cross investment strategy, in which firms invest in one another's domestic markets, deters foreign competitors from using high home-country prices to subsidize a fight for market share overseas.

E. When all barriers to entry have been eroded, multinational corporations combine production rationalization and integration with their global-scanning capability to minimize costs.

F. For many firms, becoming multinational is not a matter of choice but one of survival.
   1. If the motivating force is cost reduction, firms must search for manufacturing locations abroad which promise lower production costs in an attempt to protect eroding profit margins at home.
   2. By taking advantage of economies of scale abroad, firms can increase their customer base in order to spread high fixed costs relative to variable costs or high overhead costs over a larger quantity of sales.
   3. A policy of multiple production sites is followed by firms that fear strikes and political risk.
   4. Other firms simply enter foreign markets to gain access to information and experience (so-called knowledge seekers) that will prove to be useful in other markets.
   5. Still others, such as financial institutions, follow their customers in an effort to guarantee them an uninterrupted flow of services and goods.

G. The motives for a foreign investment may be based on factors other than profit maximization, and the benefits may accrue elsewhere in the organization. In fact, these benefits may be realized in the form of reduced risks or increased cash flows.

III. **While barriers to entry exist, they also erode over time. Thus, to remain multinational, firms must continually pursue policies and investments which are congruent with worldwide growth and survival. This approach involves five interrelated elements.**

A. The investment strategy should be geared toward building competitive advantage.

B. Individual entry strategies in foreign markets must be evaluated systematically.

C. Continual auditing should ensure the effectiveness of the current entry mode.

D. Foreign investments should be evaluated on the basis of strategic rationale.

E. Firms need to invest in developing competitive strengths that can be transferred overseas and cannot easily be duplicated by competitors.

IV. **Japanese companies begin at the low end of the market, increase production volume and global brand franchises, and then move into the high end of the market.**

A. Many U.S. companies which rely on scientific and technical research are growing in strength.

B. U.S. firms that focus on their competitive strengths and are willing to stick with their markets even when profitability declines are able to compete successfully against foreign companies.

C. Successful companies in global markets closely link R & D to market realities.

D. Japanese companies excel in industries that require incremental product improvement.

V. Appendix A discusses joint ventures as an alternative to foreign direct investment.

A.1. In some countries, particularly LDCs, the only way to penetrate the foreign market is through a joint venture with a local firm. Other joint ventures enable partners to take advantage of each other's technological strengths. Still in other cases, companies team up to share the enormous product development costs.

A.2. The advantages of a joint venture will depend on the multinational corporation's global expansion strategy. A strategy of product differentiation gives the United States firm control over the various elements of marketing. Production rationalization requires that manufacturing be concentrated in large plants in order to take advantage of economies of scale. If the supply of raw materials is important, then a joint ownership can be formed to keep out potential entrants and to prevent price cutting. Firms with high R & D expenditures to generate a diversified and innovative line of products are engaging in joint ventures so that their products can be introduced in new countries.

A.3. The decision to form a joint venture must be analyzed systematically with respect to its likely success. Not all joint ventures work out as planned, which can be attributed to conflicting objectives. Those that are forced by government regulations are unacceptable to most multinational corporations.

VI. Appendix B discusses the strategic implications of Europe 1992.

B.1. U.S. multinationals which have experience with deregulation are better able to organize their European operations along the most economically efficient lines and to redeploy assets aggressively across national boundaries.

B.2. In order to respond successfully to the challenges of a single market and stronger competition, companies must enter into cross-border alliances, merge with competitors, and otherwise restructure their operations.

B.3. Rather than pursuing scale economies across the board, corporate managements should focus on expanding only those parts of their business where economies of scales predominate.

Fill-in-the-Blanks

1. _____ _____ _____ is the acquisition by a firm of physical assets in the form of plant and equipment.

2. The value of foreign direct investment stems from projects which have _____ net present values.

3. Multinational corporations owe their existence to _____ product and/or factor markets.

4. If _____ _____ make it costly to coordinate economic activities through arm's length transactions, a firm should set up foreign operations.

5. Barriers to direct _____ _____ _____ can be advantageous to investors.

6. Multinational corporations create barriers to entry by continually _____ new products and _____ existing ones.

7. As industries reach maturity, technological know-how is replaced with _____ __ _____ and _____ __ _____.

8. When a firm's competitive advantages in its product lines or markets have dissipated, costs can be _____ by combining production shifts with _____ and _____ of its global manufacturing facilities.

9. Becoming multinational is often a matter of _____ for those firms primarily concerned about _____ in order to remain competitive.

10. A _____ home marketplace often provides a valuable _____ _____.

11. In order to stay multinational, a firm must develop competitive advantages that are _____ overseas and that are not easily _____ by competitors.

12. Over time, the _____ foreign market entry strategy is likely to _____.

Conceptual Questions

13. Foreign investments are motivated only by profit maximization.
    a. True
    b. False

14. Which of the following is/are likely to be major long-run competitive advantages of a U.S. multinational corporation?
    a. A decline in the real value of the U.S. dollar
    b. Access to low-cost foreign raw materials
    c. Its ability to quickly adapt its products and technology in line with changing market conditions
    d. All of the above
    e. None of the above

15. The acquisition of Uniroyal Goodrich by Michelin provided
    a. additional sales to U.S. automakers.
    b. entry into the private-label tire markets.
    c. entry into the associate-label tire markets.
    d. all of the above.
    e. none of the above.

16. The choice of whether to sell abroad by exporting, licensing, or foreign direct investment depends on
    a. the nature of government regulations.
    b. whether the firm's competitive advantages can be transferred abroad in the products it sells or can be written down and clearly transmitted.
    c. whether customers are looking for some signals as to the firm's commitment to the local market.
    d. all of the above.
    e. none of the above.

17. Which of the following industries would most likely take advantage of lower costs in some less developed foreign countries?
    a. Assembly line production
    b. Specialized professional services
    c. Nuclear missile planning
    d. Planning for more sophisticated computer technology
    e. None of the above

18. Joint ventures tend to be unsuitable for firms that rely heavily on a strategy of
    a. product differentiation through marketing.
    b. production rationalization.
    c. high R & D expenditures to generate a diversified and innovative line of new products.
    d. all of the above.
    e. a and b only.

19. Multinational corporations which take advantage of the learning curve can
    a. reduce taxes.
    b. reduce costs.
    c. drive out actual and potential competitors.
    d. all of the above
    e. b and c only

20. An investment strategy should be designed so that a firm is continually building competitive advantage.
    a. True
    b. False

Answers

1. Foreign direct investment

2. positive

3. imperfect

4. contractual obligations

5. international portfolio investment

6. introducing; differentiating

7. economies of scale; economies of scope

8.   minimized; rationalization; integration

9.   survival; cost

10.   competitive; competitive advantage

11.   transferable; replicated

12.   optimal; change

13.   **b.** Foreign investments are motivated by risk minimization and benefits which accrue elsewhere in the organization rather than by profit maximization only.

14.   **c.** If a firm is able to quickly adapt it products and technological processes as market conditions change, it has a major long-run competitive advantage.

15.   **d.** Michelin's acquisition of Uniroyal Goodrich was motivated by the desire to increase its presence in the North American market. For Michelin, the addition of Uniroyal Goodrich provided entry into the private-label and associate-label tire markets, from which it had been absent, and additional sales to U.S. automobile manufacturers.

16.   **d.** The selection of an optimal entry mode depends on the nature of government regulations, the firm's ability to transfer or transmit its competitive advantages abroad, and the firm's commitment to the local market.

17.   **a.** Assembly line production which requires a less skilled labor force can be easily shifted to production sites abroad, particularly where imperfections in the labor market reduce production costs (e.g., low labor costs).

18.   **a.** Where marketing is used to create barriers to entry, then control over the various elements of the marketing strategy is considered important. In this case, bringing in a local partner would likely lead to conflicts over the large advertising expenditures, channels of distribution, and pricing policies regarded optimal by the parent. However, firms have found that they can engage in a joint venture at the manufacturing stage as long as the parent company has control over quality standards and can market the goods separately through a wholly owned sales affiliate.

19.   **e.** Many multinational corporations take advantage of the learning curve in order to reduce costs and drive out competitors.

20.   **a.** In designing a global expansion strategy, firms need to be aware of those investments that are likely to be most profitable. These investments capitalize on and enhance the differential advantage the firm possesses. Thus, the optimal investment strategy should focus explicitly on building competitive advantage.

CHAPTER 18

CAPITAL BUDGETING FOR THE MULTINATIONAL CORPORATION

Overview

Capital budgeting for the multinational corporation is complicated by a number of variables which are rarely, if ever, encountered by purely domestic firms. These variables include differences between parent and project cash flows, foreign tax regulations, expropriation and blocked funds, exchange rate changes and inflation, project-specific financing, and differences between the basic business risk of foreign and domestic projects. While the net present value rule is the most appropriate decision criterion for evaluating foreign projects, adjustments must be made to incorporate the additional economic and political risks faced by the firm. Modifications can be made to either the project cash flows or the discount rate. Although the latter approach is simpler to use, it penalizes future cash flows relatively more than present ones. The firm must also take into consideration the options available to adjust the scope of a project. These options include the possibility of expanding or contracting the project or abandoning it entirely, the chance to utilize new technological processes with skills developed from implementing the project, and the possibility of entering a new line of business arising from the new project.

Outline

I. **Net present value (NPV) is the most appropriate capital budgeting technique to be used when selecting foreign investments.**

A. The net present value is defined as the present value of all expected future cash benefits discounted at an appropriate discount rate less the initial cash outlay. It is shown in mathematical terms as follows:

$$NPV = -I_0 + \sum_{t=1}^{n} \frac{CF_t}{(1+k)^t}$$

1. The discount rate, k, is the company's cost of capital which is used for projects with similar risk as the risk of the firm.
2. If the NPV is positive, the project should be accepted; if the NPV is negative, the project should be rejected.
3. If two mutually-exclusive projects are evaluated, the project with the higher NPV, given that it is positive, should be selected.

B. The most important property of the NPV technique is that it emphasizes cash flows rather than accounting profits; it focuses on the opportunity cost of funds invested; and it is consistent with shareholder wealth maximization. In addition, the NPV obeys the value additivity principle which states that the NPV of a set of independent projects is just the sum of the NPVs of the individual projects.

C. The most important and also most difficult part of any investment analysis is the estimation of cash flows. These cash flows consist of the initial cash outlay termed the net investment which occurs today (t = 0), the cash flows generated over the life of the project termed net cash flows or operating cash flows (t = 1-n), and the terminal cash flows realized in the last year of the project's life (t = n).
   1. An important principle underlying the estimation of cash flows is that these cash flows should be measured on an incremental basis. That is, only the additional cash flows from the investment need to be considered.
   2. The distinction between total cash flows and incremental cash flows is important for a number of reasons.
      a. Cannibalization occurs when an investment takes sales away from the firm's existing products.
      b. Sales creation results in additional sales for existing products.
      c. The opportunity cost, or true economic cost, of a project must be included regardless of whether the firm already owns the asset or must acquire it.
      d. Transfer prices can significantly distort a project's profitability. Thus, where possible the actual market prices should be used to evaluate the inputs or outputs of the project.
      e. Fees and royalties are expenses to the project but represent benefits to the parent firm. Only the additional costs attributable to the project should be considered. For example, overhead costs which are incurred regardless of whether the project is accepted should not be included.
   3. In general, the incremental cash flows of a project are found as the difference between worldwide corporate cash flows with and without the investment.
   4. An incremental analysis must consider the consequences of not making the investment.
   5. Intangible benefits provided by an investment in the form of valuable learning experiences and a broader knowledge base need to be incorporated into the capital budgeting process.

D. The NPV uses the firm's weighted average cost of capital (WACC) in the denominator. This discount rate is appropriate only if the foreign investment is as risky as the existing assets of the firm, and if the project is financed with the same proportions of debt and equity as the firm. However, project risk and financial structure vary by country, production stage, and position in the product life cycle.

E. The WACC can be adjusted to reflect deviations from the typical investments of the firm. An alternative approach is to discount the project cash flows at a rate that reflects only the business risk of the investment and abstracts entirely from the financing effects. This rate is called the all-equity rate which applies directly to a project that is financed only with equity.

F. The adjusted present value (APV) consists of the base case NPV in which the cash flows from the project are discounted at the all-equity rate plus the present value of any financing side effects, such as the tax shield and interest savings or penalties associated with project-specific financing. In mathematical terms, the APV is shown as follows:

$$APV = -I_0 + \sum_{t=1}^{n} \frac{CF_t}{(1+k^*)^t} + \sum_{t=1}^{n} \frac{T_t}{(1+i_d)^t} + \sum_{t=1}^{n} \frac{S_t}{(1+i_d)^t}$$

Since the tax shield and interest savings (penalties) are relatively certain, the last two terms are discounted at the before-tax dollar cost of debt.

G. Based on the capital asset pricing model, project risk is determined only by the interaction of project returns with overall market returns.

II. The foreign investment analysis raises two additional issues.

A. The cash flows from the project can differ from those remitted to the parent because of tax regulations and exchange controls.
  1. Cash flows to the parent take the form of fees and royalties, additional sales created by the project, and transfer price adjustments used to shift profits to other affiliates.
  2. Project cash flows consist of only those cash flows which are generated locally.
  3. According to economic theory, the relevant cash flows to use in determining the value of an investment will consist of only those cash flows which accrue to the investor.
  4. To simplify the foreign investment analysis, the following three-stage analysis is suggested:
     a. First, estimate and analyze the cash flows from the project's point of view.
     b. Second, evaluate the project on the basis of specific forecasts concerning the amounts, timing, and form of remittance to the parent net of any taxes or other expenses.
     c. Third, incorporate the indirect effects which are attributable to the project.
  5. The true profitability of a project is estimated by adjusting the project's cash flows for the effects of transfer pricing and fees and royalties, and for the project's strategic purpose and its impact on the rest of the organization.
  6. Because the relevant cash flows are estimated net of taxes, it is necessary to determine the amount and timing of taxes which must be paid on foreign-source income.

B. The foreign investment decision is affected by additional political and economic risks which must be incorporated into the capital budgeting analysis by adjusting either the discount rate or the payback period, or by adjusting the cash flows in each year.
  1. Raising the discount rate or shortening the payback period to reflect the added risks on a foreign investment can bias the meaning of a project's NPV.
  2. Adjusting expected future cash flows assumes that either the additional risks are diversifiable or that the foreign investment will lower the firm's market risk.
  3. When evaluating foreign projects, many firms tend to discount the most likely rather than the expected cash flows at a risk-adjusted rate.

C. Currency fluctuations and inflation can be analyzed separately when estimating a project's cash flows.

III. Political risks, such as expropriation, exchange controls, or blocked funds, can be considered by adjusting the project's expected cash flows in the NPV analysis of the project to the parent.

IV. Growth options are of great importance to multinational corporations and, thus, require an expanded NPV rule.

A. Growth options exist whenever an investment decision can be altered in response to new information and, in turn, can affect significantly the value of a project.

B. The value of an option to undertake a follow-up project, which is embodied in an investment, equals the expected NPV of the follow-up project plus the value of the option to defer or reject the project. The value of the discretion to invest or not to invest in the project depends on the length of time the project can be deferred, the risk of the project, the level of interest rates, and the proprietary nature of the option.

Fill-in-the-Blanks

1. The ___ _____ _____ is the most appropriate method for selecting investments, because it is _____ with the goal of the firm.

2. The NPV of a project is calculated by _____ the expected cash flows of the project at the company's _____ _____ ____ __ _____.

3. The cash flows of an investment should be estimated on an _____ basis and after _____.

4. Foreign production facilities may _____ existing sales or _____ additional sales for existing products.

5. _____ and _____ represent costs to the project, but are _____ from the viewpoint of the parent firm.

6. Projects with different _____ are likely to have different ____ _____ and, therefore, require a separate capital structure.

7. The _____ _____ _____ method incorporates the side effects of financing _____ and _____ __ _____ in separate terms.

8. _____ and _____ cash flows can differ substantially because of tax regulations, exchange controls, and other factors.

9. The ____ _____ of a project is determined by making various _____ to the project's cash flows.

10. The additional _____ and _____ risks faced by the MNC should be incorporated into the capital budgeting analysis by adjusting project ____ ____ instead of the _____ ____.

11. _____ __ _____ and _____ can be analyzed separately.

12. The option to _____ or ___ __ _____ in a follow-up project associated with an investment must be considered when estimating the project cash flows.

Conceptual Questions

13. A foreign project that is profitable when valued on its own can be unprofitable from the viewpoint of the parent company.
    a. True
    b. False

14. Given the differences that are likely to exist between parent and project cash flows, the relevant cash flows to use in project evaluation are the
    a. incremental worldwide cash flows received by the parent.
    b. incremental worldwide project cash flows.
    c. incremental worldwide project cash flows that can be repatriated to the parent.
    d. total worldwide cash flows generated by the project.
    e. none of the above

15. When evaluating international project cash flows, which of the following factors are relevant?
    a. Future inflation
    b. Blockage of funds
    c. Remittance provisions
    d. All of the above
    e. a and b only

16. The capital asset pricing theory is based on the premise that
    a. only unsystematic variability in cash flows is relevant.
    b. only systematic variability in cash flows is relevant.
    c. both systematic and unsystematic variability in cash flows are relevant.
    d. neither systematic nor unsystematic variability in cash flows is relevant.
    e. none of the above.

Problems

17. Suppose that with no inflation the cash flow in year 2 of a new project in Spain is expected to be Ptas. 200 million. Now suppose that Spanish inflation is expected to be 8% annually, but project cash flows are expected to rise by only 5% annually because the depreciation write-off will remain constant. If U.S. inflation is forecasted at 4% annually and purchasing power parity is expected to hold, what is the forecast dollar cash flow in year 2? The current exchange rate of the peseta is $0.01.
    a. $2.04 million
    b. $1.96 million
    c. $2.21 million
    d. $1.71 million
    e. None of the above

18. Suppose a firm projects a $5 million perpetuity from an investment of $20 million in Brazil. If the required rate of return on this investment is 20%, how large does the probability of expropriation in year 4 have to be before the investment has a negative NPV? Assume that all cash inflows occur at the end of each year and that the expropriation, if it occurs, will occur prior to the cash inflows in year 4 or not at all. There is no compensation in the event of expropriation.
    a. 15%
    b. 23%
    c. 34%
    d. 42%
    e. None of the above

Answers and Solutions

1. net present value; consistent

2. discounting; weighted average cost of capital

3. incremental; taxes

4. cannibalize; create

5. Fees; royalties; benefits

6. risks; debt capacities

7. adjusted present value; subsidies; interest tax shields

8. Parent; project

9. true profitability; adjustments

10. economic; political; cash flows; discount rate

11. Exchange rate changes; inflation

12. invest; not to invest

13. **a.** While a project may be profitable when it is evaluated in isolation, it may become unprofitable from the standpoint of the parent. The reason is that for a number of reasons project cash flows can diverge from incremental cash flows accruing to the parent.

14. **a.** The parent should value only those cash flows which can be repatriated net of any transfer costs, because only accessible funds can be used to pay dividends and interest and for reinvestment.

15. **d.** The foreign investment analysis must take into consideration political risks, such as expropriation and blocked funds, exchange rate changes and inflation, as well as the form of remittance chosen for repatriating funds back to the parent.

16. **b.** According to the CAPM theory, the market prices only systematic risk relative to the market rather than total corporate risk. Thus, only interactions of project returns with overall market returns are relevant in determining project risk.

17. **a.** Since the project cash flows will rise by only 5% annually, the cash flows in year 2 will be equal to Ptas. 200M $(1.05)2$ = Ptas. 220.5M. If Spanish and U.S. inflation are expected to be 8% and 4%, respectively, and if purchasing power parity holds, then the exchange rate in year 2 is $(1.04 / 1.08)2 \times \$0.01 = \$0.009273$ and the forecast dollar cash flow in year 2 is Ptas. 220.5M $\times \$0.009273 = \$2.04$ million.

18. **c.** The cash flow stream can be broken down into two components: one, if expropriation takes place, and another, if expropriation does not occur. The expected value of these streams is then found by multiplying the first component by the probability that expropriation will take place and the other component by the probability that expropriation will not take place.

Year	0	1	2	3	4	5+
CFs with expropriation ($)	20	5	5	5	0	0
CFs without expropriation ($)	20	5	5	5	5	5

If the probability of expropriation in year 4 is p, then the expected cash flows associated with this investment are:

Year	0	1	2	3	4	5
CFs ($)	-20	5	5	5	5 (1 - p)	5 (1 - p)

The NPV of these cash flows, discounted at 20%, is:

$$-20 + (5/1.2) + (5/1.2^2) + (5/1.2^3) + (5 (1 - p)/1.2^4) + ... + (5 (1 - p)/1.2^t) + ...$$
$$= -20 + (5/0.2) - ((5p/0.2)/1.2^3)$$
$$= -20 + 25 - 14.68p.$$

Setting this quantity equal to zero and solving for p is 34.1%. This means that the probability of expropriation must be 34% before the investment no longer has a positive NPV.

CHAPTER 19

THE COST OF CAPITAL
FOR FOREIGN INVESTMENTS

Overview

Multinational corporations will continue making foreign investments as long as there are profitable opportunities. That is, the returns earned on foreign projects must be higher than the company's required rate of return after accounting for the added economic and political risks. While most firms are aware of the risks associated with overseas investments, they simply increase or decrease the weighted average cost of capital. The issue of the cost of capital for the multinational corporation is, however, more complex than that. In the previous chapter, it was shown that the cost of capital of the firm is appropriate only in the foreign investment analysis if certain assumptions about project risk and debt capacity are made. Most projects differ in risk and capital structure which requires the estimation of a project-specific cost of capital. In addition, the interaction between the returns of the project and the outcomes of the firm's existing investments must be considered. Thus, the simple inclusion of a risk premium when evaluating foreign projects is less likely to benefit the shareholders.

Outline

I. **The cost of equity capital is the minimum rate of return that stockholders require on the firm's common stock.**

    A. An important feature of the cost of equity is that it reflects the overall riskiness of the operations the firm is involved with. Thus, the cost of equity capital can be used to value future equity cash flows and, consequently, to determine the price of the firm's common stock.

    B. The capital asset pricing model (CAPM) is a widely used method for determining the project-specific required return on equity. This model shows that an equilibrium relationship exists between the required rate of return of an asset and its risk which is represented as follows:

$$r_i = r_f + \beta_i (r_m - r_f).$$

        1. According to the CAPM, investors are compensated for only the systematic or nondiversifiable risk which is measured by beta.
        2. For a specific project, the value of beta can be found either directly from the CAPM or through professional investment companies.

    C. An alternative method for estimating the cost of equity capital is the discounted cash flow approach. Based on the dividend valuation model, the required rate of return on the equity is found as the dividend yield plus the capital gains yield, or

$$k_e = (D_1/P_0) + g.$$

D. Estimates of the required return on the equity capital, using the CAPM or the dividend valuation model, apply only to the corporate level or to investments that have similar financial characteristics as the existing assets of the firm; otherwise these estimates are useless.

II. The weighted average cost of capital (WACC) is appropriate only if the financial structures and commercial risks are similar for all investments.

A. The cost of capital for the firm is found as the weighted average of the capital components used in the firm's capital structure and their associated after-tax costs. In mathematical terms, the WACC for the parent and the project is found as

$$k_0 = (1 - L)k_e + Li_d(1 - t)$$

where L is the parent's debt ratio. The weights or proportions are based on the firm's market value target capital structure.

B. The riskiness and debt capacities projects, however, may vary from the corporate norms. Thus, it is necessary to adjust the various costs and capital components to reflect their actual values.

C. The cost of capital for a foreign project which is financed by a mix of parent company funds, retained earnings from the subsidiary, and foreign debt, is computed by first estimating the various cost components and then combining the after-tax costs with the weights of the various sources of funds.
  1. The cost on parent company funds is the firm's marginal cost of capital, k_0, provided that the foreign investment under consideration does not change the overall riskiness of the activities the multinational corporation engages in.
  2. The cost of retained earnings overseas, k_s, depends on the dividend withholding taxes, tax deferral, and transfer costs. If T is the incremental taxes owed on earnings repatriated to the parent, $k_s = k_e(1 - T)$.
  3. The after-tax dollar cost of borrowing locally, r_f, is equal to the after-tax interest cost plus the currency gain or loss.
  4. The weighted average cost of capital for the project without changes in risk characteristics equals

$$k_I = k_0 - a(k_e - k_s) - b[i_d(1 - t) - i_f]$$

where a is the weight on the subsidiary's retained earnings and b is the weight on foreign debt.

III. An alternative to adjusting the parent's cost of capital is to use the all-equity cost of capital for a foreign project.

A. The all-equity discount rate abstracts from the project's financial structure and reflects only the riskiness of the expected cash flows from the project.

B. The CAPM can be used to calculate the all-equity rate, k^*:

$$k^* = r_f + \beta^*(r_m - r_f)$$

where ß* is the beta associated with the unlevered cash flows. For example, if the beta on a foreign project is 1.25, the riskfree rate is 10%, and the return on the market is 15%, then the project's cost of capital is 16.25% [0.10 + 1.25 (0.15 - 0.10)].

C. If the riskiness of a project is similar to the risk of the average project selected by the firm, ß* can be found by unlevering the firm's stock price beta, ß$_e$, which appears in the CAPM. Unlevering can be accomplished by using the following approximation:

$$\beta^* = \frac{\beta_e}{1 + (1 - t)\, D/E}.$$

For example, if the beta of a firm's stock is 1.2, and it has a debt ratio of 50% and an applicable tax rate of 34%, then its all-equity beta is 0.90 [1.2/(1 + 0.66 x 0.5)].

IV. Project discount rates can be adjusted using the capital asset pricing model when the additional foreign risks are systematic in nature.

A. A large portion of the economic and political risks faced by a multinational corporation can be diversified away through portfolio investments at the level of the individual investor. Thus, the discount rate used for valuing foreign projects should not be affected by those risks.
   1. The systematic risk of a foreign project could be lower than that of its domestic counterpart if the economic cycles of foreign countries are less highly correlated with the home country's economic cycle.
   2. The greatest diversification benefits are provided from investments in less developed countries that have high political risk.
   3. Individual investors may be willing to pay a premium price for shares of multinational corporations which are uniquely able to diversify their portfolios internationally at lower costs than the investors could do.

B. While the capital asset pricing model is the best model of choice for estimating the cost of capital for foreign projects, the estimation of foreign subsidiary betas is much more complex. The most practical approach is to proxy foreign project betas by using the average beta for a portfolio of corporate surrogates.
   1. It is most desirable to use local companies as corporate proxies.
   2. A second alternative is to find a proxy industry in the local market.
   3. The least preferred alternative is to estimate foreign project betas by computing the U.S. industry beta for the project and then multiplying it by the unlevered foreign market beta relative to the U.S. index.

C. The relevant market portfolio for estimating a project's beta coefficient depends on whether or not capital markets are globally integrated.
   1. If capital markets are globally integrated, then the world market portfolio should be chosen.
   2. If capital markets are segmented, then the domestic portfolio is the correct choice.
   3. To be able to compare foreign projects with domestic projects, foreign project betas should be measured against the U.S. market portfolio.
   4. As a result, a foreign project's systematic risk and, hence, its cost of capital are unlikely to be higher than those of comparable domestic projects.

D. Empirical studies provide evidence that international portfolio diversification, not corporate international diversification, proves to be beneficial to shareholders.

E. To estimate the cost of equity capital for a foreign project, the relevant market risk premium to be used is the U.S. market risk premium.

V. Substantial differences exist in the cost of capital of U.S. and Japanese companies.

A. The cost of capital of Japanese corporations is almost twice as high as the cost of capital of their U.S. counterparts. This difference may be explained by the large amounts of capital which are spent on plant modernizations and research and development.
   1. U.S. companies cannot justify such enormous expenditures for new equipment, new factories, and cutting-edge research with long-term returns because of the higher cost of funds.
   2. On the other hand, Japanese companies with access to less expensive capital place less emphasis on short-term profits and focus more on investments designed to promote the creation of a dominant position in the marketplace.

B. The focus of U.S. executives on short-term profits can be traced to the reward system which stresses current period profits rather than shareholder wealth creation.

C. When U.S. interest rates are adjusted for inflation and taxes, borrowing in the United States is less expensive than obtaining financing in Japan.

D. Japanese leverage may appear high when compared to U.S. standards. But if the lower Japanese weighted average cost of capital is recomputed with market value weights using the firm's target capital structure and if allowances are made for the excess cash held by Japanese firms, the debt-to-equity ratios of Japanese companies have actually fallen and those of U.S. companies have increased.

E. Keiretsu ties provide Japanese companies with a safety net.

F. The high Japanese P/E ratios, which suggest a lower cost of capital, can be explained by the failure to take into consideration the growth in stock prices and the ownership by affiliated companies. But when the Japanese cost of equity is estimated with the CAPM and the Japanese market is deleveraged, equity risk premiums appear to be identical to those in the U.S. market.

G. Researchers have estimated that Japanese companies historically had a 1.5% to 3% cost of capital advantage.

H. Due to the collapse of the Japanese stock market combined with the sharp decline in U.S. interest rates, cost of capital differences between the United States and Japan which appeared to exist in the past have largely been eliminated.

I. Companies can cope with a cost of capital disadvantage by reducing capital intensity or increasing product differentiation.

VI. The Appendix shows how to calculate the dollar costs of long-term debt with and without taxes.

A.1. The effective dollar cost of foreign currency debt, in the absence of taxes, is found by solving for r in the following equation:

$$-Pe_0 + \sum_{i=1}^{n} \frac{r_f Pe_i}{(1+r)^i} + \frac{Pe_i}{(1+r)^n} = 0$$

If the currency is expected to change at a steady rate of g annually, both the interest expense and the principal repayment will be affected by the annual revaluation or devaluation. Thus, the present value of the cash flow per dollar of foreign currency financing discounted at r is equal to

$$-1 + \sum_{i=1}^{n} \frac{r_f (1+g)^i}{(1+r)^i} + \frac{(1+g)^n}{(1+r)^n} = 0$$

The effective interest rate, r, equals $r_f (1 + g) + g$. This is equal to the cost of a one-period foreign currency loan that devalues by an amount, g, during the period. Thus, the yield on a foreign-currency-denominated loan is equal to r_{us} if the following equation holds:

$$r_{us} = r_f (1 + g) + g.$$

A.2. The after-tax yield on a foreign-currency-denominated bond issued by a local affiliate can be found by solving the following equation for r:

$$-Pe_0 + \sum_{i=1}^{n} \frac{r_f Pe_i (1-t)}{(1+r)^i} + \frac{Pe_i}{(1+r)^n} = 0$$

Similarly, the effective after-tax cost of dollar debt is found by solving for k in the following equation:

$$-L + \sum_{i=1}^{n} \frac{r_{us} L (1-t)}{(1+k)^i} + \frac{L + t(Le_i / e_0 - L)}{(1+k)^n} = 0$$

If the foreign currency is expected to appreciate or depreciate at an annual steady rate, then the effective after-tax dollar cost on the foreign currency bond issued by a local affiliate can be found by solving the following equation:

$$-1 + \sum_{i=1}^{n} \frac{r_f (1+g)^i (1-t)}{(1+r)^i} + \frac{(1+g)^n}{(1+r)^n} = 0$$

The effective yield, r, is the same as in the single-period case adjusted for taxes:

$$r = r_f (1 + g) (1 - t) + g.$$

A simplified after-tax relationship between the dollar interest rate, r_{us}, and the foreign currency interest rate, r_{FC}, can be stated as follows:

$$r_{us} (1 - t) = r_{FC} (1 - u) (1 - t) - u$$

where u is the expected annual devaluation of the foreign currency relative to the dollar.

Fill-in-the-Blanks

1. _____ ____ for evaluating foreign projects should reflect the value to firms of undertaking specific activities.

2. The cost of capital for a project depends on the ____ of that project.

3. One approach used to estimate the _____-_____ required rate of return utilizes the _____ ____ _____ _____.

4. The company's weighted average cost of capital is appropriate only if the _____ _____ and the _____ _____ are similar for all new investments.

5. With changes in the ____ _____ of the firm, various adjustments must be made to its WACC in order to arrive at a _____ WACC.

6. The ____-_____ rate abstracts from the project's financial side effects and is based solely on the _____ ____ of the project.

7. In estimating a foreign project's cost of capital, the relevant risk component is its _____ risk.

8. _____ _____ _____ by the corporation should prove beneficial to shareholders.

9. The appropriate _____ _____ to use in estimating a project beta depends on one's view of ____ _____ ____.

10. According to conventional wisdom, the cost of capital for Japanese companies is _____ than that for U.S. companies.

11. U.S. executives focus more on ____-____ profits because of the executive ____ ____.

12. The _____ of the Japanese stock market combined with the _____ in U.S. interest rates has virtually _____ the cost of capital difference between the two countries.

Conceptual Questions

13. The rate(s) at which investors capitalize the returns on foreign projects depend(s) on
a. whether shareholders are internationally diversified.
b. the relative costs of international diversification for the MNC and for individual investors.
c. the extent to which domestic systematic risk is unsystematic from a global standpoint.
d. all of the above.

14. A foreign project's systematic risk, and, hence, its cost of capital, is unlikely to be higher than that of a comparable domestic project.
a. True
b. False

15. The cost of capital for a project in Spain should
    a. equal the parent's weighted average cost of capital.
    b. equal the required return for a similar investment in the United States.
    c. equal the minimum rate of return necessary to induce investors to buy or hold the firm's stock.
    d. equal the rate used by Spanish investors to capitalize corporate cash flows.
    e. be a function of the riskiness of the project itself.

16. There is evidence that the debt-to-equity ratio of MNCs based in
    a. the United States tend to be generally higher than MNCs headquartered in Japan.
    b. Japan tend to be generally higher than MNCs headquartered in other non-U.S. countries.
    c. the United States tend to be generally lower than companies headquartered in Japan.
    d. b and c
    e. none of the above

Problems

17. Suppose a foreign project has a beta of 0.85, the riskfree rate of return is 12%, and the required rate of return on the market is estimated at 19%. The cost of capital for the project is
    a. 16.15%.
    b. 17.95%.
    c. 19.00%.
    d. 21.23%.
    e. none of the above.

18. A firm with a corporate-wide debt-equity ratio of 1:2, an after-tax cost of debt of 7%, and a cost of equity capital of 15% is interested in pursuing a foreign project. The debt capacity of the project is the same as for the company as a whole, but its systematic risk is such that the required return on equity is estimated to be about 12%. The after-tax cost of debt is expected to remain at 7%. What is the project's weighted average cost of capital?
    a. 11.0%
    b. 8.67%
    c. 9.5%
    d. 9.7%
    e. None of the above

19. If the project's beta is 1.21, what is its unlevered beta? Assume the marginal tax rate for the firm is about 40%.
    a. 1.01
    b. 1.00
    c. 0.93
    d. 0.86
    e. None of the above

20. A U.S. multinational firm borrows British pounds for one year at 9%, and during the year expects the pound sterling to appreciate against the dollar by 2% annually. What is the approximate before-tax cost of interest in the United States?
    a. 9.0%
    b. 9.18%
    c. 11.18%
    d. 6.8%
    e. None of the above

Answers and Solutions

1. Discount rates

2. risk

3. project-specific; capital asset pricing model

4. financial structures; commercial risks

5. risk characteristics; project

6. all-equity; business risk

7. systematic

8. International portfolio diversification

9. market portfolio; world capital markets

10. lower

11. short-term; reward systems

12. collapse; decline; eliminated

13. **d.** The capitalization rate on foreign projects depends on whether shareholders are internationally diversified, the relative costs of international diversification for the MNC and for individual investors, and the extent to which domestic systematic risk is unsystematic from a global standpoint.

14. **a.** If American managers measure the beta of international portfolios against the U.S. market portfolio, then the required return on a foreign project may likely be lower, not higher, than the required returns from similar domestic projects.

15. **e.** The cost of capital for a project in Spain depends on the risk of that project.

16. **a.** During the past decade, Japanese leverage appears to have systematically fallen and U.S. leverage systematically risen.

17. **b.** The cost of capital for the project is 17.95% or

$$k^* = 0.12 + 0.85 \, (0.19 - 0.12) = 0.1795.$$

18. **b.** The weighted average cost of capital for the project is calculated as follows:

$$k_I = (1/3) \times 0.07 + (2/3) \times 0.12 = 10.33\%.$$

19. **c.** With a tax rate of 40%, the unlevered beta is 0.93, which is calculated as

$$ß_u = 1.21/[1 + (1 - 0.4)(1/2)] = 0.93.$$

20. **c.** The equilibrium dollar interest rate before taxes is 11.18% or

$$r_{us} = 0.09 (1 + 0.02) + 0.02 = 0.1118.$$

CHAPTER 20

THE MEASUREMENT AND MANAGEMENT OF POLITICAL RISK

Overview

The growing attractiveness of government intervention in the economy, for both developing and developed countries, has increased the political risks that multinational corporations have historically faced. These risks take many forms, including exchange controls, expropriation, changing tax laws and tax regulations, etc. The actions taken by the government to interfere into the workings of the economy affect the value of the firm. While the consequences are usually adverse, changes in the political environment can also provide opportunities. Thus, the need for a formal assessment of political risk and its implications for corporate decision-making is apparent. This approach can be broken down into three separate steps: (1) recognizing the existence of political risk and its likely consequences, (2) developing policies in advance to manage the possibility of political risk, and (3) developing measures to maximize the compensation of expropriated assets.

Outline

I. **Political risk can be viewed from a country-specific perspective or a firm-specific perspective.**

    A. At the macro level, firms try to forecast a particular country's political stability and attitude toward foreign investments.
       1. Political risk models used to quantify political stability in a country include both objective economic factors, such as inflation, external balances, GNP, and subjective indicators of general perceptions toward property rights.
       2. The Business Environment Risk Index (BERI) incorporates all these various economic, social, and political factors into an overall measure of the business climate, including the political environment.
       3. From an economic perspective, political risk can be defined in terms of the uncertainty over property rights. This definition includes government actions which range from outright expropriation to changes in the tax laws, thus affecting corporate cash flows and, hence, the value of the firm.
       4. One good indicator of the degree of political risk in a country is capital flight which refers to the transfer of capital abroad in response to fears of political risk.

    B. At the micro level, firms analyze whether the firm-specific activities, including both their operating and financial characteristics, are in conflict with government goals and policies.

II. **A number of social and economic factors contribute to the general level of risk in a country as a whole, also called country risk.**

A. A high government deficit is a sign of a country to be politically risky. In this case, the government makes promises to its citizens without having all the necessary funds which, in turn, may increase the propensity to expropriate property.

B. A key country risk indicator is an overvalued currency in a controlled exchange rate system. Under this regime, governments intervene in the market to fix the exchange rate by resorting to exchange controls. In addition, the constant threat of a currency devaluation encourages citizens to export their savings.

C. Another measure of potential political risk is the amount of unproductive spending in the economy. As governments use foreign capital to subsidize domestic consumption or spend it on investments yielding low rates of return, the reduced dollar-generating capability of the country make it difficult, if not impossible, to service foreign debt obligations. In this case, governments are more likely to resort to exchange controls, higher taxes, and the like.

D. A country with substantial natural, human, and financial resources is a better economic risk. By putting these resources to more efficient use, it is in a better position to achieve growth and development.

E. A country's susceptibility to external shocks depends on the financial policies and development strategies pursued by different countries. To the extent that countries can effectively deal with falling commodity prices, rising real interest rates, and rising exchange rates, governments are less likely to impose price controls, interest rate ceilings, trade restrictions, and other types of barriers.

F. Market-oriented policies improve a nation's economic health and credit worthiness.

III. **Multinational corporations structure their foreign investments in order to minimize political risk.**

A. The best approach to managing political risk is to anticipate problems and plan protective steps in advance to reduce the risk of damage from potential political and economic changes.
   1. The easiest way to deal with political risk is to avoid it by not investing in politically unstable countries.
   2. Alternatively, a company can buy insurance to cover its assets in politically risky areas. Political risk insurance can be bought from public or private insurers. In the United States, coverage is provided through the Overseas Private Investment Corporation (OPIC). This government-sponsored program offers political risk protection against loss resulting from currency inconvertibility, expropriation, and political violence. The only private insurer which covers expropriation risk is Lloyd's of London.
   3. Negotiating the environment prior to making the investment takes the form of concession agreements with the host government.
   4. Many multinational corporations minimize political risk by linking the value of their foreign operations to the parent's continued control. This can be accomplished by concentrating R & D facilities and proprietary technology in the home country, controlling the host country's transportation system, developing external shareholders, and obtaining unconditional host government guarantees for the amount of the investment.

B. After the investment has been made, the multinational corporation must develop operating policies to diminish the chances of government interference.
   1. Planned divestment involves the gradual withdrawal of the firm's equity position in the foreign investment over a fixed period of time.

2. Firms threatened with political risk may engage in short-term profit maximization by deferring maintenance expenditures, reducing marketing expenditures, eliminating training programs, producing lower-quality products, and the like.

3. Another alternative is to design a political risk management strategy that will raise the cost of expropriation to the host government. Such a program includes establishing local R & D facilities, developing export markets for the subsidiary's output, training local workers and managers, expanding production facilities, and producing a wider range of products locally as substitutes for imports.

4. A more positive strategy is to get on good terms with local individuals and groups which have an interest in the affiliate's continued existence as a unit of the parent company.

5. A radical approach to political risk management entails adapting to the inevitability of potential expropriation. In this situation, firms try to profit from their resources without owning or controlling them by entering into licensing agreements and management contracts.

IV. In the event of expropriation, the firm must develop measures to maximize compensation.

A. Rational negotiations with the host government involve persuasion that confiscation was a mistake by citing the future economic benefits the firm can provide or the disastrous consequences of not returning corporate property.

B. If negotiating with the host government does not work, the multinational corporation can try to apply pressure to get its property back.
   1. During or after the first two phases, the firm can begin to pursue legal remedies.
   2. According to the basic rule of law, legal relief must be sought first in the courts of the host country, and only after having exhausted this avenue can the company present its case in the home country or international courts.
   3. However, investors looking for indemnification from a foreign country are impeded by the doctrine of sovereign immunity and the act of state doctrine.

C. Companies which have been unsuccessful during the previous three phases will surrender to reality and attempt to salvage whatever they can from the investment.

V. Most raw material seekers active in the Third World have found themselves under considerable pressure either to divest or to participate in minority joint ventures in order to avoid outright expropriation by host governments. Alternatively, developing a multinational web of stakeholders in the foreign project can protect a company, such as Kennecott, from political risk.

Fill-in-the-Blanks

1. _____ ____ refers to uncertain actions taken by a government which will affect the value of a firm.

2. The two basic approaches used to assess political risk depend on _____ ____ analysis and on a ____ approach.

3. Political risk models include both objective _____ factors and subjective _____ of a country's attitude toward _____ _____.

4. _____ _____, such as BERI, can provide a quantitative measure of political risk.

5. One good indicator of political risk is _____ _____ which refers to the export of savings by a country's citizens.

6. Corporate susceptibility toward political risk depends on the company's _____ and _____ characteristics.

7. A country's riskiness can be evaluated by considering the _____ _____, the _____ ____ system, _____ government spending, the _____ ____, and to what extent the country will be affected by real shocks.

8. Companies can structure their _____ _____ to minimize political risk.

9. The _____ ____ _____ _____ provides low-cost political risk insurance subsidized by the U.S. government.

10. Multinational corporations that have invested in projects, can reduce their exposure to political risk by _____ all or part of their _____ interest to local investors.

11. Another alternative to minimizing political risk is to maximize _____-____ _____.

12. Through _____, a company can continue to earn profits from its resources without _____ or _____ them.

13. If negotiations with the host government prove unsuccessful, the firm can direct its _____ ____ at the government.

14. Investors must seek ____ _____ first in the courts of the ____ country.

15. Expropriation is recognized by international law as the ____ __ ___ _____ _____, provided the expropriated firm is given prompt _____ at fair market value in convertible currencies.

Conceptual Questions

16. Which of the following investments are most likely to be expropriated?
    a. An electric utility that is providing the power needed for an LDC's industrial expansion
    b. A coffee plantation that is producing beans for export under the company's brand name
    c. A TV assembly plant located in an LDC
    d. A computer plant in an LDC that is producing computers for sale abroad
    e. A fiber-glass plant that relies on rapidly evolving technology

17. The basic approach to managing political risk involves
    a. recognizing the existence of political risk and its likely consequences.
    b. developing policies in advance to cope with the possibility of political risk.
    c. in the event of expropriation, developing measures to maximize compensation.
    d. all of the above.
    e. b and c only.

18. Political risk is primarily a function of
    a. instability in the government.
    b. uncertainty over property rights.
    c. the level of violence in the society.
    d. all of the above.

19. The basic problem with the strategy of political risk avoidance is that
   a. all investments face some degree of political risk.
   b. the costs of avoidance are very high.
   c. the returns associated with tolerating political risk are very high.
   d. all of the above
   e. a and b only

20. Important country risk indicators are
   a. few natural resources.
   b. having a controlled exchange rate.
   c. being a major oil importer.
   d. all of the above.
   e. a and b only.

Answers

1. Political risk

2. country risk; micro

3. economic; measures; private enterprise

4. Country indexes

5. capital flight

6. operating; financial

7. budget deficit; exchange rate; wasteful; resource base

8. foreign investments

9. Overseas Private Investment Corporation

10. selling; equity

11. short-term profits

12. adaptation; owning; controlling

13. economic power

14. legal relief; host

15. right of the sovereign states; compensation

16. **a.** Investments which generate currency income for the host country through exports are less likely to be expropriated.

17. **d.** Managing political risk involves identifying the existence of political risk and its likely consequences, developing policies prior to making the investment to deal with the potential risk of government interference, and developing measures to maximize the compensation of expropriated firms.

18. **b.** From an economic standpoint, political risk refers to the uncertainty over property rights.

19. **a.** To the extent that all governments make decisions which influence the profitability of business, all investments, including those in the United States, face some degree of political risk.

20. **b.** In a controlled exchange rate system, the government imposes currency controls to fix the exchange rate. In addition, devaluation fears are constantly present (if the currency is overvalued), thus increasing a country's riskiness.

CHAPTER 21

INTERNATIONAL TAX MANAGEMENT

Overview

Tax planning for multinational operations is an extremely complex as well as vitally important aspect of international business. To plan effectively, the international financial manager needs to understand the tax environment and its impact on various corporate decisions.

International tax management involves using the flexibility of the multinational corporation in structuring foreign investments and remittance policies so that overall after-tax profits are maximized. Tax planning is complicated, because the amount of taxes to be paid by the firm depends on the tax systems of the home and host governments, the existence of various types of tax havens and incentives, and any bilateral tax treaties in effect. These complexities are further exacerbated by changes in current tax laws.

Outline

I. **Multinational managers need to have an understanding of the basic principles that have shaped the international tax environment.**

   A. Tax neutrality can be achieved by ensuring that corporate decisions are not affected by tax laws.
      1. Domestic neutrality in taxation involves uniformity in setting tax rates and determining taxable income, and the equalization of all taxes on profits.
      2. Foreign neutrality involves equality in taxation for a foreign-owned subsidiary of a U.S. company and a foreign-owned competitor operating in the same country.

   B. Tax equity is accomplished by ensuring that the same tax rules are applied when determining the tax burden of taxpayers in similar situations.

   C. Tax treaties represent modifications to the tax policies of multinational corporations in order to double taxation of income by two taxing jurisdictions.

II. **The U.S. government generally does not tax foreign-source income until that income is transferred to the U.S. parent company.**

   A. U.S. tax laws differentiate between branches and subsidiaries to determine where to place the tax burden.
      1. Earnings realized by a branch of a U.S. corporation are fully taxed as foreign income in the year they are generated, regardless of whether or not they are remitted to the parent firm. Branch losses, however, may be written off immediately against U.S. tax liabilities.

2. Taxes on income of foreign subsidiaries can be deferred until they are remitted to the parent in the form of dividends or payments for corporate services. Subsidiary losses will be recognized by the parent only upon liquidation of the affiliate.

B. Foreign tax credits for foreign taxes paid are granted by the United States and other home countries to avoid double taxation.
   1. A direct foreign tax credit is permitted on direct taxes imposed on the income of a foreign branch of a U.S. corporation and on foreign withholding taxes deducted from remittances to a U.S. investor.
   2. An indirect foreign tax credit is granted on dividends received by a U.S. firm from a foreign corporation in which it has an equity position of at least 10%.
   3. The indirect tax credit, which is based on the foreign income taxes already paid by the affiliate, can be calculated as follows:

$$\text{Indirect tax credit} = \frac{\text{Dividend (including withholding tax)}}{\text{Earnings after foreign income taxes}} \times \text{Foreign tax.}$$

   4. Total tax credits are limited to the U.S. tax payable on total foreign-source income for that year. Since profits in one country can be offset against losses in others, foreign income and total credits permitted are reduced. Thus, the maximum total tax credits are calculated using the following formula:

$$\frac{\text{Consolidated foreign profits and losses}}{\text{Worldwide taxable income}} \times \text{Amount of tax liability.}$$

If the overall limitation applies, a company may carry its excess foreign tax credits back two years and forward five years.

C. The Tax Reform Act of 1986 has changed the method of taxing foreign-source income of U.S. multinational corporations.
   1. Five new and distinct baskets or limitations have been created to calculate tax credits separately for controlled foreign corporations' minority foreign subsidiaries.
   2. For deemed remittances, a new method, called look thru, was introduced which re-categorizes earnings remitted from a controlled foreign corporation (CFC) based on the nature of the underlying income of the CFC and then places it into the separate FTC limitation baskets.

D. Expenditures are allocated and foreign tax credits calculated according to the location of income generated by these expenditures.
   1. By allocating more expenses incurred in the United States against foreign-source income, FTC limitations will be reduced as well as the deductibility of foreign taxes paid. The calculation of the maximum total tax credits is affected by this reallocation in the following way:

$$\frac{\text{Taxable income from foreign sources}}{\text{Taxable income from all sources}} = \frac{\text{Maximum foreign tax credit}}{\text{U.S. tax liability before foreign tax credit}}.$$

2. Note that the IRS reallocation, which lowers the maximum foreign tax credit available, will generate more actual FTCs.

E. Intercompany transactions adjusted by the IRS result in arm's length transactions to reflect the income that has actually been generated by the foreign affiliate.

F. U.S. multinational corporations must pay taxes on their Subpart F income even if that income is not remitted to the United States.

G. According to the excess passive assets rule of Section 956A of the 1993 Tax Act, a portion of the current income of a controlled foreign corporation that owns passive income-producing assets exceeding 25% of its total assets, is treated as deemed-paid dividends and must be included in U.S. taxable income whether or not it has been remitted to the United States.

III. **U.S. multinationals receive tax incentives for setting up foreign sales corporations and U.S. possessions corporations.**

A. The Tax Reform Act of 1984 created the Foreign Sales Corporation (FSC) which is the U.S. government's primary tax incentive for exporting goods produced in the United States into overseas markets.

B. A small FSC is generally the same as an FSC with the exception that the small FSC is not required to meet the foreign management and foreign economic process requirements.

C. A U.S. possessions corporation is entitled to numerous tax benefits which take the form of tax-exemptions of foreign-source income, tax-free repatriation of earnings to the U.S. parent firm, more liberal transfer pricing rules, and the like. The 1993 Tax Act, however, has substantially scaled back these benefits.

IV. **Multinational corporations can use tax havens and their form of corporate organization to shield income from taxes.**

A. Tax-haven countries are countries characterized by moderate levels of taxation and liberal tax incentives. Thus, multinational corporations that channel income through these countries are able to substantially reduce or defer their taxes.

B. In addition to selecting a tax haven, the firm must decide whether to set up its operation there in the form of a branch, a subsidiary, or a tax incentive corporation. The decision of the form of organization depends on three factors:
1. The projected cash flows in the country under consideration.
2. The attitude of the U.S. parent firm with regard to repatriating funds.
3. The alternative uses of funds.

V. **The form of taxation used predominantly outside of the United States is the value-added tax (VAT).**

A. The value-added tax is an indirect tax that is levied on the value added at each production stage.
1. The main economic effect of this type of tax is to encourage the expansion of highly profitable firms since the tax falls more heavily on low-income than on high-income firms.
2. The amount of tax paid is the same regardless of the form of business.

B. A simpler method of indirect taxation is a retail sales tax.

C. In the future, most countries are likely to switch from the personal income tax to either a retail sales tax or a value-added tax which is expected to result in increased savings and investments, automatic indexation of taxes for inflation, and improved trade competitiveness.

VI. **The organizational form to be used abroad must be carefully analyzed taking into consideration the objective of the firm and the cash flows of the particular foreign unit under consideration.**

A. The basic decision to be made about the organizational form centers on whether to use a branch or an incorporated subsidiary. The actual choice depends on the alternative uses of foreign tax credits.

B. Other possible forms of organization include the FSC, U.S. possessions corporation, and tax-haven corporations.

C. The optimal form of organization overseas may change over time, depending on profitability and other factors.

Fill-in-the-Blanks

1. _____ have a significant impact on the financing and investment decisions of a firm which, in turn, will affect its _____.

2. The objective of _____ ___ _____ is to _____ global after-tax profits.

3. A _____ ____ is one that will not affect any aspects of the investment decision.

4. Tax equity insures that income from a _____ branch is taxed in the same manner as income from a _____ branch.

5. ___ _____ and ___ _____ _____ are designed to avoid double taxation of foreign-source earnings.

6. In the United States, _____-_____ income is not taxed until it has been received by the parent firms.

7. For tax purposes, a distinction is made between _____ and _____.

8. The _____ _____ rule on tax credits states that the credit for foreign taxes paid cannot be _____ than the U.S. tax payable on total foreign-source income.

9. Under the look-thru rules, if all income from a CFS is operating income, then all payments received by the parent will be deemed _____ _____.

10. In calculating the foreign tax credit, the U.S. _____ __ _____ ____ must be applied to determine the foreign-source taxable income of U.S. companies.

11. Subpart F income is _____ even if that income is not transferred to the U.S. parent.

12. Multinational corporations which set up their foreign activities as a _____ _____ _____ or a U.S. _____ _____ will receive tax incentives from the U.S. government.

13. The 1993 Tax Act has substantially _____ the benefits U.S. possession corporations have been entitled to.

14. Earnings channeled through ___-____ countries are subject to ____ taxation and more _____ tax incentives.

15. The value-added tax is an _____ tax levied at each stage of production but only on the _____ _____ at that specific stage.

16. The form of organization depends on the _____ of the firm and the ____ _____ from the foreign subsidiary under consideration.

Conceptual Questions

17. What corporate decisions can be affected significantly by taxes?
    a. Foreign investment decisions
    b. Managing exchange rate risk
    c. Determining financing costs
    d. All of the above
    e. a and c only

18. Tax planning would not be necessary if tax rules were identical among all countries.
    a. True
    b. False

19. A transfer pricing strategy would likely attempt to transfer earnings from a subsidiary in a _____ country to a subsidiary in (a) _____ country.
    a. high tax; another high tax
    b. low tax; high tax
    c. low tax; another low tax
    d. high tax; low tax
    e. None of the above

20. What is the role of tax planning by the multinational corporation?
    a. Knowing the tax laws of each country
    b. Using the tax laws to analyze the feasibility of alternative policies
    c. Determining the value of the firm
    d. All of the above
    e. a and b only

Answers

1. Taxes; value

2. international tax management; maximize

3. neutral tax

4. foreign; domestic

5. Tax treaties; foreign tax credits

6. foreign-source

7. branches; subsidiaries

8. overall limitation; greater

9. operating income

10. source of income rules

11. taxable

12. foreign sales corporation; possessions corporation

13. reduced

14. tax-haven; lower; liberal

15. indirect; value added

16. objectives; cash flows

17. **d.** Taxes have a significant impact on areas as diverse as foreign investment analysis, exchange rate management, determining financing costs, and the like.

18. **b.** Even if the tax laws among countries are identical, tax planning is important because these tax laws are subject to changes in each year.

19. **d.** Transfer pricing can be used by multinational corporations to reduce their overall tax liability by imposing high prices and interest rates on goods or funds transferred to those subsidiaries located in high-tax countries.

20. **e.** Financial executives with tax responsibilities need to understand the tax environment with its various tax laws and basic principles and its impact on corporate decisions.

CHAPTER 22

INTERNATIONAL FINANCING AND
INTERNATIONAL FINANCIAL MARKETS

Overview

As capital markets grow closer internationally and corporations become more sophisticated, the search for financing is no longer restricted to one nation or financial market. This is particularly true for the multinational corporation which has access to a wide range of external sources of capital. These include commercial banks, export financing agencies, public (government) financial institutions, development banks, and private and public placement of bonds and stocks. While many of these financing sources are internal to the countries in which the firm operates, an increasing amount of funds is being raised in the Eurocurrency and the Eurobond markets. These offshore markets can offer attractive financing at relatively low costs because of government regulations and taxes elsewhere. However, the growing amounts of funds flowing between the Eurocurrency markets and the domestic markets make government intervention increasingly irrelevant.

Outline

I. **A number of sources of financing exist in financial markets.**

   A. Firms can raise funds internally or externally.
      1. Internal financing is generated from the operations of the firm in the form of reinvested earnings.
      2. External financing can come from issuing bonds or stocks in the capital market. These financial securities are generally negotiable and take the form of debt or equity.
      3. Alternatively, a firm can raise funds through commercial bank loans or by privately placing bonds. Unlike publicly issued bonds, privately placed bonds are issued to a limited number of investors, are generally nonnegotiable, and have covenants ranging from limits on the payment of dividends to prohibitions on sales of assets and issues of new debt.

   B. Different countries have different financing patterns.
      1. In Japan, companies rely heavily on outside sources of funds..
      2. In Europe and the United States, internal financing has consistently played an important role in supplying the funds needed.
      3. Regardless of the countries in which corporations operate, debt financing is preferred over equity financing as the external source of capital.

   C. Securitization, which involves replacing bank loans with securities issued in public markets, is increasing everywhere. This trend largely reflects the reduction in cost of accessing financial markets at the same time that the cost of bank borrowing has increased.

D. The globalization of financial markets, which stems from advances in communication and technology combined with financial deregulation, has further reduced the cost of issuing new securities.

E. Freer markets together with widely available information have provided the basis for global growth which is further fueled by innovation.
   1. Financial innovation segments, transfers, and diversifies risk.
   2. It creates financial market imperfections, enabling companies to access previously unavailable markets and permits investors and issuers to take advantage of tax loopholes.
   3. It also increases international capital mobility.

F. International securitization is replacing financial intermediation as the costs of gathering information on foreign firms continue to decline.

II. **The primary function of a financial market is the efficient transfer of funds from savers to investors that have productive investment opportunities.**

   A. International financial markets typically develop in countries characterized by political stability and minimal government interventions.
      1. The most important international financial centers are located in London, Tokyo, and New York.
      2. World financial centers serve as entrepots or channels through which funds are passed from nonresident suppliers of funds to nonresident users of funds. These important regional centers with unimportant domestic financial markets are located in Switzerland, Luxembourg, Singapore, Hong Kong, the Bahamas, and Bahrain.

   B. Multinational corporations have access to local financial markets in those countries in which they operate and in countries whose capital markets are open to world competition.
      1. The foreign bond market is that portion of the domestic bond market that represents issues floated by foreign companies or governments.
      2. The foreign banking market is that portion of the domestic banking market which supplies bank loans to foreigners abroad.
      3. The foreign equity market is that portion of the domestic equity market that places foreign equity issues. Placing stock in foreign markets offers benefits to the selling company.
         a. The equity funding risk can be diversified.
         b. The potential demand for a company's shares can be increased by attracting new stockholders.
         c. A global shareholder base can be built.

   C. The long-term risk to the global economy caused by abrupt shifts in capital flows and continuous currency devaluations is that some politicians will seek to reimpose controls on capital and trade flows.

III. **The most important international financial markets are those based on Eurocurrencies.**

   A. The Eurocurrency market is composed of several large banks that accept deposits and make loans in foreign currencies.
      1. Deposits in dollars or other freely convertible currencies placed in a bank in Europe or on other continents become Eurocurrencies.
      2. The Eurobond market differs from the Eurocurrency market in that Eurobonds are issued directly by the final borrower. In the Eurocurrency market, investors hold short-term

claims on commercial banks which, in turn, act as intermediaries to transform these deposits into long-term claims on final borrowers.

3. The growth of the Eurodollar market can be partially attributed to various government policies.

    a. U.S. regulations in 1968 limited the amount of foreign lending by U.S. banks. Thus, foreign affiliates of U.S. parent companies had to obtain U.S. dollar financing from banks in Europe.

    b. Ceilings imposed on the interest rates of dollar deposits in the United States motivated the transfer of dollars to the Eurodollar market where such government regulations were nonexistent.

    c. Moreover, reserve requirements on dollar deposits were not mandated for Eurobanks. Thus, banks could reduce the spread between the rates paid on these deposits and charged on loans and still earn a reasonable profit.

    d. Taxes imposed on interest earned on foreign debt sold in the United States significantly increased the cost of borrowing in the U.S. capital markets by foreign corporations and governments.

4. Due to continued domestic deregulation, the U.S. money market and the Eurodollar market are now tightly integrated, thereby eroding the cost and return differentials experienced in the past.

5. Eurocurrency transactions involve a chain of deposits between the original dollar depositor and the U.S. bank, and the transfer of control over the deposits from one Eurobank to another.

6. Eurocurrency loans are made on a floating-rate basis.

    a. The basic borrowing rate is set at a fixed margin over LIBOR for a given period and currency chosen.

    b. Periods or rollover periods are typically six months in length with the possibility of shorter periods of one or three months.

    c. The margin between the cost of funds to the lending bank and the rate charged on the loan depends on the perceived riskiness of the borrower.

    d. Maturities can vary from three to ten years with longer terms becoming the norm rather than the exception.

    e. The drawdown of the loan and the repayment period vary with the borrower's needs.

7. An increasing amount of Eurodollar loans include a multi-currency clause which gives the borrower the option to switch from one currency to another on any rollover date. This option enables firms to match their foreign-currency-denominated cash inflows and cash outflows, thereby reducing exchange rate risk.

8. Interest rates in national and international markets are closely linked through the arbitrage activities of investors who would borrow funds in the low-cost market and invest these funds in the high-return market, thereby eliminating any interest differentials.

9. As a result of the narrower spreads in the Eurocurrency market, banks can offer attractive deposit rates to corporations and governments with excess funds and attractive lending rates to corporations and governments with needs for funds.

B. Eurobonds are bonds sold outside the country in whose currencies they are denominated.

    1. Over the past decade, the Eurobond market has experienced substantial growth approaching the size of the Eurocurrency market.

    2. A major cause of this dramatic development has been the use of swaps which are financial instruments giving two parties the right to exchange streams of income over time.

    3. Due to arbitrage activities between the domestic dollar and Eurobond markets, much of the interest rate disparity that used to exist in these two markets has been eliminated.

    4. Eurobond issues are typically arranged through an underwriting group involving a hundred or more underwriting banks. An increasing number of Eurobonds is placed

privately because of the simplicity, speed, and privacy with which private placements can be arranged.

5. While the U.S. dollar was the dominant currency in the Eurobond market, other currencies, such as the German mark, and currency baskets, most notably the European Currency Unit (ECU), have become important substitutes.

6. Because of the rising demand of investors to sell Eurobonds prior to maturity, a Eurobond secondary market has developed which adds liquidity to the market.

7. Eurobonds with maturities of seven years or more must be retired by setting up a sinking fund or a purchase fund. In addition, most Eurobonds carry a call provision.

8. A major reason for the growth and survival of the Eurobond market is that investors and issuers are able to avoid government regulations and controls as well as certain taxes. However, as financial deregulation continues and U.S. withholding taxes on interest paid to foreigners are eliminated, the attractiveness of the Eurobond market will diminish.

C. Eurocurrency loans and Eurobonds differ from each other in five ways.

1. Interest rates on Eurobonds can be both fixed and variable, while for Eurocurrency loans, it is only variable.

2. The maturities of Eurobonds are still longer than those for Eurocurrency loans.

3. The size of Eurobond issues is approaching that of the Eurocurrency market.

4. The multi-currency clause and drawdown period on a floating-rate loan make it a more flexible source of funds than the issuance of Eurobonds.

5. Borrowers known internationally can raise capital in the Eurocurrency market very quickly, while placing a Eurobond issue takes more time.

D. A note issuance facility (NIF), which is a low-cost substitute for syndicated credits, allows borrowers to issue their own short-term notes. It is placed and distributed by financial institutions that provide the NIF.

E. Euronotes differ from floating-rate notes (FRN) in several ways.

1. Euronote issuers can draw down part or all of their total credit as needed and can also roll over portions of it.

2. They can determine the timing of the issue, depending on the prevailing interest rates in the market.

3. Maturities and rollover periods can be tailored to the needs of the borrower.

4. Investors must be willing to hold Euronotes until maturity, since a secondary market does not exist.

F. A growing number of firms are bypassing financial intermediaries by issuing Euro-medium-term notes to the market directly.

G. The Eurocurrency market can be broadly defined to include banks in Asia which accept deposits and make loans in foreign currencies, also referred to as the Asiacurrency market. Located in Singapore, this market has grown rapidly due to the lack of government regulations there. Its primary function is to channel to and from the Eurodollar market the large pool of offshore funds, mainly U.S. dollars, circulating in Asia.

IV. **The United States and other countries have established a variety of development banks which help finance projects that otherwise would not be funded with private capital.**

A. The most important development bank is the World Bank Group which consists of the International Bank for Reconstruction and Development (IBRD), the International Development Association (IDA), and the International Finance Corporation (IFC).

B. Regional development banks finance industrial, agricultural, and infrastructure projects which are considered important to the economic development of underdeveloped areas.

C. Development banks build up the public sector at the expense of the private sector which, in turn, may hamper economic growth.

D. Recognizing the role of development banks and the growing importance of the private sector in furthering economic growth, the Baker plan calls for development aid only if borrowers pursue free-market policies to encourage private enterprise.

V. The appendix illustrates a Eurocurrency loan agreement.

Fill-in-the-Blanks

1. Firms have three general sources of funds available: _____-_____ funds, ____-____ _____ funds, and ____-___ _____ funds.

2. The _____ _____ of companies in different countries vary from one another.

3. _____ reflects the increased use of accessing financial markets directly for funds.

4. The globalization of financial markets stems from advances in _____ and _____ combined with _____ _____.

5. _____ _____ segments, transfers, and diversifies risk.

6. Foreigners are often hampered to access domestic capital markets because of _____ _____.

7. The _____ ___ _____ is that part of the domestic bond market that represents issues _____ by foreigners.

8. _____ _____ are being increasingly sold in foreign markets.

9. A Eurocurrency is a dollar or other _____ _____ currency deposited in a bank _____ its country of origin.

10. The _____ market thrives because of government regulations elsewhere.

11. Eurocurrency loans are made on a _____-___ basis.

12. _____ activities ensure that the _____ in interest rates between the domestic and the international money markets are quickly _____.

13. A _____ is a bond that is sold in countries other than the country in whose currency it is denominated.

14. The Eurobond market exists because investors are able to avoid _____ _____ and _____.

15. Some Eurobonds called _____-___ ____ have a variable rate provision that adjusts the coupon rate over time according to prevailing market interest rates.

16. _____ banks provide financing for projects whose economic benefits cannot be completely captured by _____ _____.

17. Economic growth is _____ since development banks build up the _____ sector at the expense of the _____ sector.

18. The _____ _____ calls for development aid only if borrowers pursue policies that support private enterprise.

Conceptual Questions

19. Eurodollar deposits represent the liabilities of
    a. European non-financial corporations.
    b. the Organization of Petroleum Exporting Countries.
    c. European banks and U.S. bank branches abroad.
    d. European banks exclusively.
    e. none of the above.

20. Suppose the French government imposes an interest rate ceiling on French bank deposits. What is the likely effect of this regulation?
    a. Reduce Eurofranc interest rates
    b. Raise Eurofranc interest rates
    c. Have no effect
    d. Cannot tell

21. Ghana is seeking concessionary financing to build one hundred schools. Which of the following agencies is most likely to provide such financing?
    a. The World Bank
    b. The International Monetary Fund
    c. The International Finance Corporation
    d. The International Development Agency
    e. None of the above

22. Suppose that the current 90-day London Interbank Offer Rate is 11%. If next period's LIBOR is 10.5%, then a Eurodollar loan priced at LIBOR plus 1% will cost
    a. 12% this period and 11.5% next period.
    b. 11% this period and 10.5% next period.
    c. 12% this period and 12% next period.
    d. 11% this period and 11% next period.
    e. none of the above.

23. Eurocurrency spreads are narrower than in domestic money markets, because
    a. Eurobanks are not required to maintain reserves on Eurodollar deposits.
    b. Eurobanks face lower regulatory expenses.
    c. national banks are often required to lend money to certain borrowers at concessionary rates.
    d. all of the above.
    e. a and b only.

24. The most important change in Japanese corporate finance in recent years has been the shift from internal funds to bank loans.
    a. True
    b. False

25. Investors and borrowers are attracted to ECU bonds.
    a. True
    b. False

Answers

1. internally-generated; short-term external; long-term external

2. financing patterns

3. Securitization

4. communications; technology; financial deregulation

5. Financial innovation

6. government regulations

7. foreign bond market; floated

8. Equity issues

9. freely convertible; outside

10. Eurocurrency

11. floating-rate

12. Arbitrage; differences; eliminated

13. Eurobond

14. government regulations; taxes

15. floating-rate notes

16. Development; private investors

17. hampered; public; private

18. Baker plan

19. **c.** Eurodollar deposits can be placed in a foreign bank or in the foreign branch of a domestic bank.

20. **a.** If the French government imposes an interest rate ceiling on French bank deposits, holders of French francs will shift some of their deposits into the Eurofranc market to earn a higher rate. As the supply of Eurofrancs rises relative to the demand for francs, the Eurofranc interest rate should decline.

21. **d.** IDA is authorized to make highly concessionary loans for projects which are most likely to be of benefit to the host country. This would be the case when providing financing for the one hundred schools in Ghana.

22. **a.** Eurodollar loans are made on a floating-rate basis, with the rate set at a fixed margin over LIBOR. Thus, if next period's annualized LIBOR is 10.5%, then the Eurodollar rate will be at 11.5% (10.5% + 1%) on an annualized basis.

23. **d.** Eurocurrency spreads are narrower than in domestic money markets because of the lack of reserve requirements on dollar deposits and lower regulatory expenses. In addition, Eurobanks are not forced to lend money to certain borrowers at concessionary rates.

24. **b.** In recent years, almost 70% of Japanese corporate funds has come from internal rather than external sources. This switch from internal to external financing since 1973 demonstrates the maturity of Japanese industry.

25. **a.** Issuing ECU bonds has several benefits to the issuer and the investor, including (1) access to markets that might not otherwise be available, (2) diversification of currency risk, especially for investors and borrowers in the European Monetary System, and (3) a hedge against the dollar.

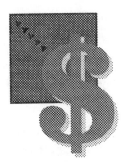

CHAPTER 23

SPECIAL FINANCING VEHICLES

Overview

Multinational corporations use special financing instruments to achieve various objectives. For example, funding foreign operations through interest rate and currency swaps and bank loan swaps provides the opportunity to reduce financing costs and/or risk. Alternatively, debt-to-equity swaps can be used to retire some of the local debt of hard-pressed less developed countries and can also provide inexpensive financing for plant expansions.

Outline

I.   **Interest rate swaps are used to hedge interest rate risk, while currency swaps are used to hedge exchange rate risk.**

    A. An interest rate swap is an agreement between two parties to exchange U.S. dollar interest rate payments for a specific maturity on an agreed-upon notional amount.
        1. In a coupon swap, one party pays a fixed rate which is calculated at the time of trade as a spread to a particular Treasury bond; the other party pays a variable rate that is adjusted periodically during the life of the agreement according to a designated index.
        2. In a basis swap, two parties agree to exchange floating-rate interest payments based on different reference rates.
        3. While swaps have risk-reducing potential, they are also used to reduce costs. Their ability to do so for both parties depends on the difference in perceived credit quality across financial markets.

    B. Interest rate swaps arranged across currencies are called currency swaps. In this arrangement, two parties exchange foreign-currency-denominated financial debt obligations at periodic intervals.
        1. The economic purpose of a currency swap is similar to a parallel loan.
        2. However, currency swaps differ from parallel loans in a variety of ways.
           a. A currency swap is not a loan. Thus, no interest is involved, and no record of the transaction appears on the balance sheets of the contracting parties.
           b. In addition, the right to offset any non-payment of interest and principal with a comparable non-payment is more firmly established.
        3. Compared to interest rate swaps, currency swaps involve exchanging the principal amounts at maturity at a predetermined exchange rate.
        4. As in parallel loans, the exchange market is completely circumvented both at the inception and the reversal of the transaction. The exchange rate is used only as a reference to determine the amounts to be exchanged.

5. The exchange of principals at maturity in a currency swap further offsets the interest differential between the currencies.

C. An interest rate/currency swap, also called a cross-currency interest rate swap, is designed to convert a liability denominated in one currency with a stipulated type of interest payment into one denominated in another currency with a different type of interest payment.

D. A dual currency bond swap involves swapping fixed dollar payments in the future for fixed payments stated in foreign currency in the future. This type of swap is a variation of the currency swap.

E. Swaps provide economic benefits to both parties when barriers to arbitrage exist. These impediments must take the form of legal restrictions on currency transactions, different perceptions by investors of risk and credit worthiness of the contracting firms, attractiveness of one borrower to a certain class of investors, tax differentials, and the like.

II. **Multinational corporations use international leasing to avoid or defer taxes.**

A. There are two common types of leases: operating and financial leases.
  1. An operating or service fee includes both maintenance and financing services.
    a. An operating lease separates the ownership and use of the asset.
    b. The lease agreement is written for less than the asset's useful life; that is, the lease is not fully amortized.
    c. The lease can be renewed on a period-by-period basis.
    d. Operating leases often contain a cancellation clause to protect the lessee against obsolescence.
  2. A financial lease or capital lease is fully amortized. However, they do not provide maintenance and are not cancelable.
    a. In a financial lease, economic ownership resides with the lessee. Thus, a financial lease is equivalent to borrowing money and buying the asset.
    b. Lease payments are financial fixed obligations, in that default by the lessee may result in bankruptcy.

B. Lease payments are tax-deductible expenses provided the lease qualifies as a true lease and is not a disguised installment sale.
  1. If the lease is tax-oriented, the lessor receives the tax benefits associated with owning the asset, and the lessee can deduct the full value of the lease payments.
  2. If the lease is a financial lease, the lease payments cannot be fully deducted because these payments are treated as installments of the purchase price plus interest. As the economic owner, the lessee is allowed tax depreciation for the purchase price and a tax deduction for the interest factor. The lessor, however, cannot enjoy the benefits of ownership and is taxed on the interest which is part of the lease payment.
  3. If an international lease is structured as a double-dip lease, both the lessee and the lessor are permitted by both countries to realize the tax benefits of ownership.
  4. If additional parties are involved in an international lease, such as a financial institution or a sublease in a third country, each will be entitled to capital allowances.

C. By incorporating an international leasing company in an appropriate location, the multinational corporation can achieve various objectives. These include shifting income from high-tax countries to low-tax countries, reducing or eliminating withholding taxes on lease payments, bypassing exchange controls, and avoiding expropriation.

D. A recent innovation in the international leasing business has been the introduction of yen-based leases called Shoguns. A Shogun lease enables leasing companies with the help of U.S. banks to circumvent capital controls imposed by Japan's Ministry of Finance. As a result, lease financing can be provided for longer-term capital investments involving large sums of money.

III. The market for LDC debt-equity swaps has grown rapidly in recent years.

A. Under a debt-equity program, investors purchase the external debt of a less developed country on the secondary market at a discount and then swap it into local equity.

B. A debt-peso swap enables domestic investors to purchase their country's foreign debt at a discount and then to convert this debt into local currency.

C. Although debt swaps help reduce a country's external debt, it can fuel the already high rate of inflation of those countries participating in this arrangement.

D. On the other hand, debt swaps may lead to additional capital formation in a country and, if combined with a privatization program, have no inflationary impact.

Fill-in-the-Blanks

1. _____ are low-cost financing instruments which increase a corporation's control over _____ ___ risk and _____ _____.

2. An interest rate swap is an _____ between two firms to exchange U.S. dollar _____ _____ for a specific _____ on an agreed-upon _____ principal amount.

3. While interest rate swaps can be used to _____ interest rate risk, they may also be used to _____ costs.

4. A _____ ____ is an agreement between two parties in two separate _____ to exchange an equivalent amount of two different _____ which is _____ at an agreed upon future date.

5. Since a currency swap ___ ___ create foreign currency denominated receivables or payables, _____ and _____ exposure are avoided.

6. A currency swap involving a _____ _____ _____ is one that has the issue's proceeds and interest payments stated in foreign currency and the principal repayment stated in dollars.

7. Swaps will provide only _____ _____ to the contracting firms if _____ exist that prevent arbitrage from functioning fully.

8. International leasing can be used to ____ and ____ taxes, safeguard an affiliate's _____, and circumvent _____ _____.

9. A ___-_____ lease grants tax benefits of ownership to the _____ and ____ ___ _____ of lease payments to the _____.

10. In a double-dip lease, both parties are treated as the ____ of the leased asset for ___ purposes.

11. Multinational corporations can achieve certain _____ by incorporating an _____ _____ _____ in an appropriate _____.

12. ____ _____ enable investors to obtain domestic currency assets at a _____.

13. The result of governments purchasing their external debt is to increase the already high ____ __ _____.

Conceptual Questions

14. The theoretical principal underlying the swap is called the
    a. basis amount.
    b. swap differential.
    c. notional principal.
    d. arbitrage principal.

15. A currency swap is equivalent to a
    a. currency option with the exercise price equal to the current spot rate.
    b. long-dated forward foreign exchange contract where the forward rate is the current spot rate.
    c. interest rate swap, where the basis is the differential between the fixed and floating interest rate.
    d. short-term currency futures contract.
    e. none of the above

16. LDC bank loans trade at deep discounts to their face value, because
    a. investors believe they will not be repaid in full.
    b. investors must pay high taxes on their capital gains.
    c. the LDCs often impose stringent currency controls.
    d. all of the above.
    e. a and b only.

Problems

17. Company A, a low-rated firm, desires a fixed-rate, long-term loan. A presently has access to floating interest rate funds at a margin of 1.5% over LIBOR. Its direct borrowing cost is 13% in the fixed-rate bond market. In contrast, company B, which prefers a floating-rate loan, has access to fixed-rate funds in the Eurodollar bond market at 11% and floating-rate funds at LIBOR + 0.5%. Suppose they split the cost savings. How much would A pay for its fixed-rate funds?
    a. 11%
    b. 12.5%
    c. 13%
    d. 13.5%
    e. None of the above

18. How much would B pay for its floating-rate funds?
    a. LIBOR + 1.5%
    b. LIBOR + 1.0%
    c. LIBOR + 0.5%
    d. LIBOR
    e. None of the above

19. Chrysler has decided to make a $100 million investment in Mexico via a debt-equity swap. Of that $100 million, $20 million will go to pay off high-interest peso loans in Mexico. The remaining $80 million will go for new capital investments. The government will pay 86 cents on the dollar for debt used to pay off peso loans and 92 cents on the dollar for debt used to finance new investments. If Chrysler can buy Mexican debt in the secondary market for 60 cents on the dollar, how much will it cost Chrysler to make its $100 million investment?
    a. $66,127,402
    b. $110,212,336
    c. $23,255,814
    d. $86,956,522
    e. None of the above

Answers and Solutions

1. Swaps; interest rate; currency exposure

2. agreement; interest payments; maturity; theoretical

3. hedge; reduce

4. currency swap; countries; currencies; reversed

5. does not; translation; transaction

6. dual currency bond

7. economic benefits; barriers

8. defer; avoid; assets; currency controls

9. tax-oriented; lessor; full tax-deductibility; lessee

10. owner; tax

11. objectives; international leasing company; location

12. Debt swaps; discount

13. rate of inflation

14. **c.** The term notional refers to the theoretical principal underlying the swap. Thus, the notional principal is simply a reference amount against which the interest is computed.

15. **b.** In a currency swap, principal amounts are always exchanged at maturity at a predetermined exchange rate. The swap contract, therefore, behaves like a long-dated forward exchange contract, where the forward rate is the current spot rate.

16. **a.** LDC debt trades at deep discounts to their face value to reflect the market's opinion that it will not be repaid in full.

17. **b.** Based on the numbers presented, there is an anomaly between the two markets: One judges that the difference in credit quality between the two firms is worth 200 basis points, whereas

the other determines that this difference is worth only 100 basis points. The parties can share among themselves the difference of 100 basis points by engaging in a currency swap. This transaction would involve A borrowing floating-rate funds and B borrowing fixed-rate funds and then swapping the proceeds. If they split the cost savings, A would pay 12.5% for its fixed-rate funds.

Party	Normal Funding Cost	Cost After Swap	Difference
A	13.00%	12.50%	0.50%
B	LIBOR + 0.5%	LIBOR	0.50%

18. **d.** B would pay LIBOR for its floating-rate funds.

19. **a.** Chrysler will need $20,000,000/0.86 = $23,255,814 in face value debt to buy enough pesos to pay off the $20 million peso loan. It will need another $80,000,000/0.92 = $86,956,522 to acquire the $80 million in pesos it must have for its capital investment. These amounts sum to $110,212,336 ($23,255,814 + $86,956,522) in face value bank loans. At a price of 60 cents on the dollar in the secondary market, Chrysler will have to pay $66,127,402 ($110,212,336 x 0.60) for this face amount of bank debt.

CHAPTER 24

DESIGNING A GLOBAL FINANCING STRATEGY

Overview

In order to take advantage of market distortions, reduce operating risk, and establish a worldwide capital structure, the multinational corporation must select an appropriate financing strategy for its international operations. Some of the major variables to be considered include the firm's debt-to-equity mix, taxes, exchange rate risk, diversification of sources of capital, the ability to move funds without government interventions across borders, various capital and exchange controls imposed by foreign authorities, and government subsidies. The nature of the eventual financing strategy chosen is potentially at odds with corporate objectives, such as minimizing financing cost, reducing economic exposure, ensuring funds availability, and reducing political risk. Thus, the choice of trade-offs to be made in arranging global financing requires an explicit analytical framework.

Outline

I. **Firms can create value by arranging below-market financing.**

   A. Raising funds at concessionary rates stems from government-induced financial market distortions.

   B. Tax asymmetries lead to the possibility of lower after-tax costs by carefully selecting securities.
      1. Zero-coupon bonds, which pay no interest, are sold at a deep discount to their face value. The discounted price and amount received at redemption may vary in different capital markets, thus providing investors an opportunity to gain from such differences.
      2. Parent company financing of foreign subsidiaries in the form of debt rather than equity has certain tax advantages.

   C. Multinational corporations are in a unique position to take advantage of government credit and capital controls. The ability to access a variety of sources and types of capital and to shift funds with their internal transfer system enables multinational corporations to secure the lowest risk-adjusted cost money and to bypass credit restraints.

   D. Many governments offer incentives and subsidies to multinational corporations to influence their production and export sourcing decisions.
      1. Export financing agencies provide loans at concessionary rates with long repayment periods and with low-cost political and economic risk insurance.
      2. Firms engaged in import projects can obtain financing from governments at attractive low rates with long repayment periods.

3. Regional banks and international development banks are potential sources of low-cost, long-term, fixed-rate funds for certain types of investments.

E. Special financing instruments can be designed by firms that attract funds at a cost less than the market's required rate of return on comparable risk securities.

II. Excessive risk-taking can adversely affect a firm's relations with its non-investor stakeholders.

A. Firms should arrange their financing in such a way that the risk exposures are kept at manageable levels if the cost of doing so is not too high.

B. Exchange rate risk can be reduced by hedging the exposure.

C. Political risk can be minimized by financing projects with funds from various governments, development banks, and customers.

D. Product market risk can be managed by selling goods in advance to customers.

E. The firm's operational flexibility and ability to respond quickly to competitive intrusions depend on assuring access to funds. This can be accomplished by maintaining unused debt capacity and liquid assets, diversifying the sources of funds internationally, and buying insurance indirectly through excess borrowing.

III. When the multinational corporation establishes its capital structure, the focus must be on the consolidated, worldwide financial structure.

A. In selecting the proper mix of debt and equity for the entire corporation, a multinational corporation is able to use more debt in its capital structure than a purely domestic firm without increasing the risk of bankruptcy because of the earnings diversification provided by its foreign operations.

B. The issue of a proper foreign subsidiary capital structure is complicated by a number of factors. Questions arise as to whether the financial structure of affiliates should conform to that of the parent company or to local norms, or whether it should vary so as to take advantage of opportunities to minimize the parent firm's cost of capital.
   1. If the parent company finances its affiliates by raising capital in its own country and then investing these funds as equity, the debt ratio of overseas operations would be zero.
   2. If the parent company invests only one dollar of share capital in each subsidiary and requires all to finance operations on their own, with or without guarantees, the affiliate debt ratio would approach 100%.
   3. If the parent company itself borrows the funds and then relends the monies in the form of intercorporate loans to its affiliates, the debt ratios of foreign subsidiaries would be close to 100%.
   4. In each of these three cases, the amount of borrowing and the debt-equity mix of the consolidated corporation are identical.
   5. Thus, the optimal capital structure for a subsidiary is completely distinct from the firm's overall debt ratio.

C. An individual subsidiary has no independent capital structure unless the parent allows its foreign affiliate to default on its debt.

D. The financial risk of the overall corporation is not determined by the degree of financial leverage of its affiliates. Moreover, having affiliate capital structures conform to parent or local norms is unrelated to shareholder wealth maximization. Thus, the capital structure decision for foreign subsidiaries is irrelevant.

  1. The Tax Reform Act of 1986 has complicated the choice of financing for multinational corporations, because the distribution of debt between the parent company and its affiliates affects the use of foreign tax credits.
  2. A multinational corporation using international leasing can increase the allowable foreign tax credit on foreign-source income.
  3. If the global capital structure is determined on the basis of minimizing cost, then subsidiaries with access to low-cost funds would be allowed to exceed the parent company capitalization norm, and subsidiaries located in higher-capital-cost nations would have lower target debt ratios.
  4. Some companies require their foreign units to be financially independent in order to motivate them.

E. Joint ventures complicate the financing decision because of significant conflicts that may arise between the U.S. company and its local partner.

Fill-in-the-Blanks

1. Selecting an appropriate _____ strategy for the multinational corporation involves a ____-___ between the availability of the different financing _____ and the relative ____ and effects of the sources on the firm's _____ ____.

2. Financing options at _____ market rates create value.

3. Below-market financing results from financial market _____ caused by _____, government _____ and _____ _____, and government _____ and _____.

4. Multinational corporations can take advantage of _____ _____ to lower their cost of funds.

5. _____ ___-_____ can adversely affect a firm's relations with its customers, employees, and other stakeholders.

6. Firms should arrange their _____ to reduce ____ if the cost of doing so is not excessively high.

7. The risk of currency _____ can be minimized by appropriately arranging the affiliate's financing.

8. To ensure access to funds, a multinational corporation needs to maintain substantial _____ debt capacity and _____ assets.

9. A key element of the global financing strategy is to _____ financing sources _____.

10. In establishing a multinational corporation's capital structure, the focus must be on the corporation's _____, _____ financial structure.

11. A subsidiary does not have a _____ capital structure unless the parent allows its affiliate to _____.

12. The _____ of subsidiary capital structures is recognized by many multinational corporations.

13. The _____ of where to finance foreign operations has been complicated by the passage of the ___ _____ ___ of 1986.

14. Some companies _____ their foreign affiliates to stand on their own feet to _____ them.

15. The financing decision of a _____ _____ is complicated by the different interests pursued by the U.S. company and the local partner.

Conceptual Questions

16. Capital structures of foreign affiliates should
    a. conform to the standards set by local companies.
    b. vary so as to take advantage of opportunities to reduce overall risk and financing costs.
    c. be very similar to the parent's capital structure because this is what determines the firm's risk profile.
    d. conform to the standards established by other foreign units.
    e. none of the above

17. Companies can use financing to inspire confidence among their customers, employees, and other stakeholders by
    a. taking advantage of low-cost financing sources.
    b. using substantial amount of debt to take full advantage of the interest tax shield.
    c. using minimal debt in the capital structure.
    d. all of the above.
    e. a and b only.

18. Low-cost export financing is often a bad sign.
    a. True
    b. False

19. A company producing oil overseas for export can best reduce its risk by
    a. borrowing in the local currency to reduce currency risk.
    b. using take-or-pay contracts for the oil it produces.
    c. financing its investment with a maximum amount of equity.
    d. all of the above.
    e. a and b only.

Problems

20. Suppose that the cost of borrowing restricted French francs is 7% annually, whereas the market rate for these funds is 12%. If a firm can borrow FF 10 million of restricted funds, how much will it save annually in before-tax franc interest expenses?
    a. FF 500,000
    b. FF 700,000
    c. FF 1,000,000
    d. FF 1,200,000
    e. None of the above

21. Suppose that Taiwan offers GM a 5-year, $30 million loan at 9% interest to set up a local production facility. The principal is to be repaid at the end of the fifth year. The market interest rate on such a loan is about 20%. With a marginal tax rate of 40%, how much is this loan worth to GM?
    a. $7.3 million
    b. $7.8 million
    c. $7.1 million
    d. $11.2 million
    e. None of the above

Answers and Solutions

1. financing; trade-off; sources; costs; operating risk

2. below

3. distortions; taxes; credit; capital controls; subsidies; incentives

4. export financing

5. excessive risk-taking

6. financing; risk

7. inconvertibility

8. unused; liquid

9. diversify; internationally

10. consolidated; worldwide

11. separate; default

12. irrelevance

13. choice; Tax Reform Act

14. force; motivate

15. joint venture

16. **b.** The objective of the capital structure decision is to determine that mix of debt and equity for the parent and all its consolidated and unconsolidated subsidiaries which will maximize shareholder wealth. This can be accomplished best by allowing foreign subsidiary capital structures to vary in order to take advantage of opportunities that will minimize the multinational corporation's cost of capital.

17. **c.** Companies can inspire sufficient trust and confidence in customers, employees, and other stakeholders by minimizing the amount of debt used to finance foreign operations. As a result, the firm will be seen as financially sound and viable over the long run.

18. **a.** A country that has a comparative advantage in the manufacture of certain products does not need to provide subsidies, such as low-cost financing, to stimulate exports of those products. Its cost advantage will suffice. Thus, the fact that a nation feels it must subsidize export sales to be competitive could indicate that it is a high cost producer. Of course, the possibility always exists that the country is cost-competitive but uses subsidies to counter the subsidies that foreign competitors receive.

19. **b.** By using a take-or-pay contract, the firm sells its expected output in advance to its customers on the basis of mutual advantage. The purchaser benefits by having a stable source of supply, usually at a discount from the market price. The seller benefits by having an assured outlet for its products which protects against product market risk and a contract that can be discounted at a consortium of banks.

20. **a.** The annual interest savings on FF 10 million of restricted funds at 7% when the market rate is 12% equals FF 10,000,000 (0.12 - 0.07) = FF 500,000.

21. **c.** By borrowing at 9% when the market rate is 20%, GM saves 11%. This translates into annual before-tax savings of $30,000,000 (0.20 - 0.09) = $3,300,000. With a marginal tax rate of 40%, this yields annual after-tax savings of $3,300,000 (1 - 0.40) = $1,980,000. The value of this 5-year annuity, discounted at GM's after-tax cost of debt of 0.20 (1 - 0.40) = 12% is $1,980,000 × 3.6048 = $7,137,504.

CHAPTER 25

INTERNATIONAL BANKING TRENDS AND STRATEGIES

Overview

With expanding international trade and the emergence of the multinational corporation, the demand for international financial services increased. Banks located in the traditional financial centers responded by following their customers and extending loans to governments with promising economic policies. Lending to governments of less developed countries represented the fastest growing category during the 1970s. This trend continued until economic conditions in the industrialized countries changed, and the demand for goods from the LDCs subsided. Thus, with lower export earnings, the regularly scheduled payments for servicing the foreign debt could not be met. As a result of the sudden drying up of inflows of funds, international banks pulled back sharply on their lending. Although the international debt crisis has eased off, the international banking activities continue to be depressed.

Banks follow their customers overseas in order to extend services to the foreign operations of their commercial clients. They have several options in their overseas expansion which include branching, local bank acquisitions, and representative offices. If the volume of business in another country is not substantial, most banks will rely on correspondent banking relationships or make use of domestic organizational forms, such as the Edge Act and Agreement Corporations and international banking facilities. Each of these entry strategies has its advantages and disadvantages which must be carefully evaluated.

Outline

I. **International banking has grown rapidly in both complexity and risk over the past two decades.**

A. The evolution and growth of international banking can be largely attributed to the growth of international business. Many banks expanded overseas to retain the domestic business of customers who made foreign investments by expanding and improving the scope of their activities abroad.

B. With the onset of the energy crisis in late 1973, a great need for recycling funds from oil-exporting to oil-importing nations was created. International banks were able to provide the services needed, because they had the broad experience in international lending, and they received large shares of OPEC's surplus revenues in the form of deposits.

C. Bank lending to the governments of less developed countries represented the fastest growing category of international bank loans during the 1970s and early 1980s. In 1982, however, the international financial markets were hit with troubles when a number of developing countries announced that they were unable to service their foreign bank debt. With the beginning of the debt crisis, lending to LDCs quickly dried up.

D. By 1983, the intensity of the international debt crisis has eased off. World economies were recovering from recession, and many loan rescheduling negotiations had been completed successfully.

E. Although international lending activities have picked up, they continus to be depressed compared to the high growth period of the late 1970s because of (1) the inability of LDC debtor nations to achieve sustained economic growth, and (2) the use of equity capital instead of new bank lending to finance strong economic growth as experienced by some LDCs.

F. To ensure the safe operation of all banks worldwide, a well-defined supervisory structure must be established. Bank regulators are setting international bank regulations which address two additional issues: (1) the lender of last resort, and (2) the institution responsible for monitoring internationally active banks.

G. In late 1987, the Bank for International Settlements in Basel, Switzerland, developed standards against which to measure capital adequacy. Under the agreement, banks must achieve a minimum 8% risk-based ratio of capital to assets by the end of 1992. In order to meet these standards, banks are focusing more on profits and less on growth.

H. More recently, Japanese banks have greatly expanded their overseas loan portfolios but are now in the process of pulling back. This retrenchment may be explained by the financial adversity toward Japanese investments at home and the new risk-based capital standards which are changing the way Japanese banks are doing business abroad.

II. **Banks have several options in their overseas expansion which, in turn, have important implications for the range, cost, and efficiency of services provided.**

A. The way a bank should approach its foreign markets is influenced by a number of variables, including the overall financial resources, the level of experience with each market, the volume of international business, and the strategic plans of the bank.

B. A great majority of banks maintain correspondent relationships or banking arrangements with local banks worldwide. Their main function is to help provide financing for the foreign subsidiaries of their multinational corporate clients.
   1. Advantages: (a) Low cost form of market entry; (b) no investment in staff or facilities; (c) benefits derived from having multiple sources of business given and received; (d) referrals to local banking opportunities; (e) ability to take advantage of correspondent's local knowledge and contacts.
   2. Disadvantages: (a) U.S. customers may be given low priority by correspondents; (b) certain types of credit may be difficult to arrange because of capital restrictions; (c) credit may not be provided regularly and extensively by the correspondent.

C. A bank opens up representative offices to provide advisory services to banks and customers and to speed up the services of correspondent banks. They also help generate loan and deposit business for the American parent bank but are not authorized to directly accept deposits or make loans. Thus, customers dealing with the representative office are actually doing business with the bank located in the home country of the bank.

1. Advantages: (a) Low-cost entry to foreign markets; (b) efficient delivery of services provided the volume is small; (c) attracting additional business; (d) preventing losses of existing business.
2. Disadvantages: (a) Inability to penetrate the foreign market more effectively; (b) expensive since capital is not generated; (c) difficulty in attracting qualified personnel.

D. A true international banking presence can be accomplished by establishing a foreign branch of the American bank. A branch is able to conduct all of the activities associated with a representative office, and it is authorized to accept deposits and make loans. Overseas branching is preferred by American banks because of the follow-the-customer rationale, the direct contribution to bank earnings, and the greater access to overseas financial markets.
   1. Advantages: (a) Greater control over foreign operations; (b) greater ability to offer direct and integrated services to customers; (c) greater ability to manage customer relationships.
   2. Disadvantages: (a) High-cost form of entry into a foreign market; (b) difficult and expensive to train branch managers.

E. An alternative to establishing a foreign branch is to acquire a foreign bank which is then operated as a separate subsidiary.
   1. Advantages: (a) Immediate access to local deposit markets; (b) ability to utilize an established network of local contacts and clients.
   2. Disadvantages: (a) Expensive; (b) highly risky; (c) difficult to make work effectively.

F. Edge Act and Agreement Corporations are U.S. bank subsidiaries that can carry on international banking and investment activities.
   1. Edge Act Corporations are physically located in the United States. Their activities are limited to international operations. Customers can be either foreigners or Americans. Edge Act bank deposits and loans, however, must be internationally related and cannot be used for domestic purposes.
   2. An Agreement Corporation is functionally similar to the Edge Act Corporation. Usually, it is state-chartered and enters into an agreement with the Federal Reserve to limit its activities to those of an Edge Act Corporation.

G. International banking facilities (IBFs) can conduct international banking activities exempt from U.S. regulation.
   1. IBFs are merely bookkeeping entities that represent a separate set of asset and liability accounts of their establishing offices.
   2. Their major activities are deposit-taking and lending to foreign individuals and large foreign business firms subject to the same regulations as foreign banks.
   3. Because IBFs do not transact domestic banking business, they are exempt from reserve and deposit insurance requirements and interest rate limitations, such as Regulation Q.
   4. IBF operations are closely linked to the Eurocurrency markets, as evidenced by the high proportion of both assets and liabilities due to other banking institutions.

H. Foreign banks have greatly expanded their U.S. activities in recent years. This growth can be attributed to several factors, including the rapid growth of U.S. international trade, the size and importance of U.S. financial markets, the growth of foreign direct investment in the United States, and the role of the U.S. dollar as an international medium of exchange.

I. The completion of a single European market by the end of 1992 will enable banks to branch throughout the European Community and offer a greater range of financial services. A single banking license will lower bank costs by using common distribution networks, managers, and support systems, and by eliminating overlapping or conflicting standards and regulatory procedures.

III. International banks can use various strategies to create value in their marketplace.

A. Well-capitalized banks can gain a competitive advantage by underwriting securities and providing low-cost loans to customers. The larger the capital base, the more profitable will be their business relationships.

B. International banking can help develop a competitive advantage by having an organization that is able to exploit information to learn and to innovate more quickly than competitors. Such a strategy involves making investments in human resources; that is, preparing and enabling people to recognize and respond to customer problems. This also requires investment in information technology necessary to identify customer problems and create new services and products to solve them.

C. To be able to compete successfully in complex global markets, banks must be willing to invest large amounts of money in information systems. Since the benefits of information acquisition and transfer are so great, only those banks with a firm commitment to providing a global service are likely to undertake it.

D. Companies with foreign operations are demanding endless services around the world, including a transfer agent who can pull together all transactions on a global, integrated basis. Thus, transaction-processing services, such as movement of funds, foreign exchange, international cash management, letters of credit, etc., can be very profitable bank services. To accommodate multinational business customers, banks are required to make substantial investments in a state-of-the-art information system. While economies of scale are significant, market share is critical.

E. During the 1990s, global competition in international banking will intensify. To be successful, banks must be able to shift to the trading of currencies, securities, and derivative products. They must also be able to manage the complex risks inherent in these financial markets. The major competitors include European, Japanese, and U.S. banks which have important competitive strengths and weaknesses.

Fill-in-the-Blanks

1. International banks have grown rapidly during the 1970s by _____ _____.

2. The fastest growing category of international bank lending were loans to governments of ____ _____ _____.

3. International banking was hit hard in the summer of 1982 when several LDCs announced that they were _____ to make the regularly scheduled _____ on their _____ to international creditors.

4. ___ _____ denominated loans made borrowers vulnerable to the increases in the real value of the dollar.

5. With the onset of the _____ ____ ____, international banks pulled back sharply on their _____ _____.

6. _____ _____ and _____ _____ provide low-cost entry to foreign markets.

7. The costs of _____ _____ are much higher but provide greater _____ to local markets.

8. _____ a local bank provides _____ access to the local markets, but most acquirers tend to _____.

9. Edge Act and Agreement Corporations are _____ of U.S. banks that are permitted to carry on _____ _____ and _____ activities.

10. _____ _____ _____ can conduct international banking activities which are exempt from U.S. regulation.

11. In recent years, _____ ___ _____ in the United States has grown substantially.

12. International banks can use several _____ to create _____ in the marketplace.

Conceptual Questions

13. For many international banks, their initial ventures overseas were
    a. designed to overcome limitations imposed by the Glass-Steagal Act.
    b. designed to exploit arbitrage opportunities presented by the Eurocurrency market.
    c. defensive in nature.
    d. all of the above.
    e. a and b only.

14. The smaller the volume of business overseas, the more likely a bank is to rely on _____ to handle their needs in a foreign country.
    a. branch banks
    b. correspondent banking
    c. acquisition
    d. representative offices
    e. none of the above

15. Foreign bank acquisitions tend to be
    a. expensive.
    b. highly risky.
    c. relatively unprofitable.
    d. all of the above.
    e. a and b only.

16. The most important advantages of IBFs are that
    a. they do not have to keep a percentage of their deposits in non-interest-bearing accounts at the Federal Reserve.
    b. deposits in IBFs are not subject to interest rate ceilings or deposit insurance assessment.
    c. they can take both foreign and domestic deposits in any amounts.
    d. all of the above are important advantages.
    e. a and b only

Answers

1. recycling petrodollars

2. less developed countries

3. unable; payments, debts

4. U.S. dollar

5. international debt crisis; international lending

6. Correspondent banking; representative offices

7. foreign branches; access

8. Acquiring; immediate; overpay

9. subsidiaries; international banking; investment

10. International banking facilities

11. foreign bank activity

12. strategies; value

13. **c.** Many banks ventured overseas to retain the domestic business of customers who invested abroad. Their motive was primarily defensive in nature.

14. **b.** Until the volume of business in another country is substantial, most banks will choose to rely on correspondent banking relationships.

15. **d.** Most banks make the mistake of paying too much for their foreign acquisitions which are highly risky and generally not worthwhile unless the acquirer has more to contribute to the acquisition than money.

16. **e.** IBFs are exempt from U.S. regulation, such as reserve and deposit insurance requirements and interest rate limitations on deposits.

CHAPTER 26

THE INTERNATIONAL DEBT CRISIS AND COUNTRY RISK ANALYSIS

Overview

U.S. banks rushed into international lending because of the higher returns that could be earned on loans to foreigners compared with those from domestic loans. To minimize the risks associated with international lending, several safeguards were built into the loans and the operations of international banks. And for many years, it was believed that they were successful. However, recent developments have suggested otherwise. With the event of the international debt crisis in the early 1980s, many banks found themselves confronted with a sudden interruption of inflows of funds due to the repayment problems on past loans. In addition, new sources of funds were drying up, thereby reducing the pool of capital to be loaned out.

As a result of the debt crisis, banks have reevaluated their lending policies and made adjustments to insulate themselves from a recurrence of the crisis. A first step in learning from the crisis is to determine its causes. A second step involves assessing a country's ability to make loan payments on external debt. In fact, an accurate country risk assessment would have indicated in advance the potential debt-repayment problems of borrowers.

Outline

I. **In the early 1980s, the international banking environment was severely affected by the inability of several large borrowers to repay their international loans on time.**

   A. Several key contributing factors led to the development of the international debt crisis which began in the early 1980s.
      1. Banks with large deposits from OPEC surplus revenues participated in international bank lending to governments presiding over promising national economies. A vast majority of LDC loans was made on a floating-rate basis and denominated in the U.S. dollar, thus making borrowers highly vulnerable to increases in real interest rates and in the real value of the dollar.
      2. In 1979, OPEC implemented an oil price increase which resulted in increased balance-of-payments deficits of the lesser developed countries and an increased need of LDCs for external financing.
      3. This crisis was further fueled by the economic policies of the industrial countries in general, and the United States in particular, designed to deal with rising inflation. The combination of an expansionary fiscal policy and a tight monetary policy led to sharply rising real interest rates in the United States and, consequently, in the Eurocurrency market where most of the international bank loans were funded.

4. With the global recession in the industrial countries during the early 1980s, the demand for LDC products was reduced and, thus, the export earnings used to meet the loan repayments.

B. In August 1982, Mexico announced that it was unable to meet the regularly scheduled payments on its external debt, followed by Brazil and Argentina. By the spring of 1983, about 25 LDCs could not meet their debt payments as scheduled and had entered into loan rescheduling negotiations with their creditor banks.

C. In October 1985, U.S. Treasury Secretary James Baker called on LDCs to undertake growth-oriented structural reforms supported by increased financing from the World Bank and commercial banks. The goal of the Baker Plan was to improve LDC economic growth which, in turn, would make these countries more desirable borrowers and restore their access to international capital markets.

D. Since the promised policy changes and economic performance could not be delivered on time, banks felt threatened that they might be forced into large write-offs on their existing loans. In May 1987, Citicorp responded by increasing its loan loss reserves, followed by other banks.

E. In 1989, a new plan was initiated to emphasize debt relief through forgiveness instead of new lending. The Brady Plan offered banks two choices: Banks (1) could either make new loans, or (2) could write off portions of their existing loans in exchange for new government securities whose interest payments were backed with money from the IMF. In order for this plan to work, however, banks would have to make loans at the same time as existing ones were written off.

F. The sudden emergence of debt renegotiations began in the early 1980s. While net financial transfers were reduced to levels consistent with desired economic growth, the LDCs still needed external financing in order to achieve this growth. However, banks' willingness to supply the necessary funds was hindered by their doubts about the debtor nations' ability and willingness to make sound economic policy.

G. Although debt burdens have worsened the economic problems of debtor countries, all too often the underlying causes could be found in the patronage-bloated bureaucracies, overvalued currencies, massive corruptions, and politically motivated investments in unproductive ventures.

H. Ten years after it began, the decade-long Latin American debt crisis ended in July 1992, when Brazil signed an agreement to restructure it $44 billion debt owed to foreign banks. In the end, genuine economic reforms, not negotiations, ended the debt crisis.

II. **A country risk assessment can indicate in advance the potential debt-repayment problems of borrowers.**

A. Domestic commercial loans differ from loans to foreign governments in two ways.
   1. Loan covenants cannot be easily enforced if the borrower is a sovereign state.
   2. Economic and financial policies imposed by foreign banks are often not accepted by sovereign states.

B. Since banks have great difficulty in enforcing their international loan contracts, they syndicate the loans and include cross-default clauses. Thus, the penalty for repudiation is much stiffer because a larger number of banks will now deny credit to the borrower in the future.

C. A country's ability to repay external loans depends largely on its ability to generate export revenues in U.S. dollars and other hard currencies. This ability, in turn, is based on the nation's terms of trade defined as a weighted average of its export prices relative to its import prices.
1. Thus, if the terms of trade increase, the country is a better credit risk.
2. The terms of trade risk is increased if the government tries to avoid making the necessary economic adjustments to the country's changed wealth position.

D. The speed with which a country implements necessary austerity policies will be determined by the costs and benefits associated with austerity compared to default.
1. The cost of austerity is determined by the nation's external debt relative to its wealth position, as measured by GNP.
2. The cost of default is measured by the possibility of being denied international credit.
3. Highly variable terms of trade and an unstable political system increase the odds that a government will be tempted to hold off any necessary adjustments, thus magnifying country risk.

E. The risk associated with a nation's debt burden can be measured by coverage ratios, such as the debt service-to-exports ratio and debt service-to-GNP ratio.

Fill-in-the-Blanks

1. _____ refers to the possibility that a foreign borrower is unable to service or repay the external debts to its international creditors.

2. Rising _____ in the United States combined with increased _____ boosted the LDCs' net interest payments to foreign banks.

3. The negotiations of _____ the debtor nations' loan payments began in 1980.

4. The _____ called on LDCs to undertake growth-oriented structural reforms, while the _____ emphasized debt relief through forgiveness instead of new lending.

5. Banks have great difficulty in ensuring the _____ of their international debt contracts.

6. If countries default on their foreign debts, they may be _____ of the capital markets.

7. _____ on a country's debt partly depends on ___ the government responds to a change in its _____.

8. ____-_____ ensure that a default to one bank is a default to all banks.

9. The ____ a nation's terms of trade _____ and the ____ stable its _____, the ____ its country risk.

10. The ____ ____-__-____ and ____ ____-__-___ ratios can be used to measure the risk associated with a nation's debt burden.

Conceptual Questions

11. Rapid inflation would ordinarily be expected to
    a. raise the interest rates on Eurodollar loans
    b. reduce the export revenues of LDCs
    c. raise world output
    d. all of the above
    e. a and b only

12. The international banks cut lending to LDC debtors after 1982 because of
    a. a sudden drying up of funds from OPEC.
    b. the difficulty the LDC debtor nations were having in achieving sustained economic growth.
    c. uncertainties as to the capacity of LDC debtor nations to service their existing debt.
    d. all of the above.
    e. a and c only.

13. When the nation's terms of trade declines, the government will
    a. face political pressure to maintain the nation's standard of living.
    b. often fix the exchange rate at its former level.
    c. need additional external financing.
    d. all of the above.
    e. none of the above.

14. The cost of default depends on
    a. the likelihood of being cut off from international credit.
    b. the nation's geopolitical importance to the United States.
    c. the stability of the nation's political system.
    d. all of the above.
    e. b and c only.

15. The possibility of mass defaults is the real international debt crisis.
    a. True
    b. False

Answers

1. Country risk

2. real interest rates; indebtedness

3. rescheduling

4. Baker Plan; Brady Plan

5. enforceability

6. frozen out

7. Default risk; how; terms of trade

8. Cross-default clauses

9.   more; fluctuate; less; political system; greater

10.   debt service-to-exports; debt service-to-GNP

11.   **e.** High U.S. inflation led to sharply rising real interest rates in the United States and in the Euromarkets where banks funded most of their international loans. Furthermore, a recession in the industrial countries reduced the demand for the LDCs' products and, thus, reduced the export earnings needed to service their international bank debt.

12.   **d.** Confronted with interruptions in inflows of funds due to repayment difficulties on their past loans, with the drying up of new sources of funds, and with the growing uncertainties as to the capacity of their borrowers to service their debt, the international banks pulled back sharply on their lending.

13.   **d.** When a nation's terms of trade decline, the government will face political pressure to maintain the nation's standard of living. A typical response is to fix the exchange rate at its former and now overvalued level. Moreover, the deterioration in the trade balance results in added government borrowing.

14.   **d.** The cost of default is the possibility of being cut off from international sources of funds which brings with it its own form of austerity. Most nations will follow this path as a last resort, preferring to stall for time in the hope of being bailed out. The bailout decision, which is largely political, depends on the willingness of the citizens of another country to tax themselves on behalf of the country involved. This willingness, in turn, is a function of the nation's geopolitical importance to the United States and the probability that the necessary economic adjustments will not result in unacceptable political turmoil.

15.   **a.** The threat to cut off credit to borrowers who default is meaningful only as long as banks have sufficient resources to reward those with additional credit who do not default. But if several countries default simultaneously, the banks' capital bases will be eroded and no further credit can be provided to those borrowers who repay their debts. As a result, even the latter group of borrowers will suffer from a reduction in credit. Thus, the lesser penalty for defaulting may induce borrowers to default en masse. In fact, the possibility of such mass defaults would constitute the real international debt crisis.